*Mecklern
Internet World*™

60 Minute Guide to the Internet

Including the World-Wide Web

Mecklermedia's official Internet World™

60 Minute Guide to the Internet
Including the World-Wide Web

Andrew Kantor

internet WORLD™

IDG Books Worldwide, Inc.
Foster City, CA • Chicago, IL • Indianapolis, IN • Braintree, MA • Dallas, TX

Mecklermedia's Official Internet World™
60 Minute Guide to the Internet Including the
World-Wide Web
Published by

IDG Books Worldwide, Inc.
An International Data Group Company
919 East Hillsdale Boulevard, Suite 400
Foster City, CA 94404

Mecklermedia　　**Mecklermedia Ltd.**
20 Ketchum Street　Artillery House, Artillery Row
Westport, CT 06880　London, SW1P 1RT, UK

Copyright
Copyright © 1995 by Mecklermedia Corporation. All rights reserved. No part of this book (including interior design, cover design, and illustrations) may be reproduced or transmitted in any form, by any means, (electronic, photocopying, recording, or otherwise) without the prior written permission of the publisher and copyright holder. For authorization to photocopy items for internal corporate use, personal use, or for educational and/or classroom use, please contact: Copyright Clearance Center, 222 Rosewood Drive, Danvers, MA 01923 USA, Fax Nbr. 508-750-4470.

Library of Congress Catalog Card No.: 95-077584
ISBN 1-56884-342-9
Printed in the United States of America
First Printing, September, 1995
10 9 8 7 6 5 4 3 2 1
Distributed in the United States by IDG Books Worldwide, Inc.

Limit of Liability/Disclaimer of Warranty
The author and publisher of this book have used their best efforts in preparing this book. IDG Books Worldwide, Inc., International Data Group, Inc., Mecklermedia Corporation, and the author make no representation or warranties with respect to the accuracy or completeness of the contents of this book or the material on the disk included with this book, and specifically disclaim any implied warranties of merchantability or fitness for any particular purpose, and shall in no event be liable for any loss of profit or any other commercial damage, including but not limited to special, incidental, consequential or other damages.

Trademarks
All brand names and product names used in this book are trademarks, registered trademarks, or trade names of their respective holders. IDG Books Worldwide, Inc. and Mecklermedia Corporation are not associated with any product or vendor mentioned in this book.

Published in the United States

Welcome to the world of IDG Books Worldwide.

IDG Books Worldwide, Inc. is a subsidiary of International Data Group, the world's largest publisher of computer-related information and the leading global provider of information services on information technology. IDG was founded more than 25 years ago and now employs more than 7,500 people worldwide. IDG publishes more than 235 computer publications in 67 countries (see listing below). More than fifty million people read one or more IDG publications each month.

Launched in 1990, IDG Books Worldwide is today the #1 publisher of best-selling computer books in the United States. We are proud to have received 3 awards from the Computer Press Association in recognition of editorial excellence, and our best-selling ...For Dummies™ series has more than 18 million copies in print with translations in 24 languages. IDG Books, through a recent joint venture with IDG's Hi-Tech Beijing, became the first U.S. publisher to publish a computer book in the People's Republic of China. In record time, IDG Books has become the first choice for millions of readers around the world who want to learn how to better manage their businesses.

Our mission is simple: Every IDG book is designed to bring extra value and skill-building instructions to the reader. Our books are written by experts who understand and care about our readers. The knowledge base of our editorial staff comes from years of experience in publishing, education, and journalism — experience which we use to produce books for the '90s. In short, we care about books, so we attract the best people. We devote special attention to details such as audience, interior design, use of icons, and illustrations. And because we use an efficient process of authoring, editing, and desktop publishing our books electronically, we can spend more time ensuring superior content and spend less time on the technicalities of making books.

You can count on our commitment to deliver high-quality books at competitive prices on topics consumers want to read about. At IDG, we value quality, and we have been delivering quality for more than 25 years. You'll find no better book on a subject than an IDG book.

John Kilcullen
President and CEO
IDG Books Worldwide, Inc.

IDG Books Worldwide, Inc. is a subsidiary of International Data Group, the world's largest publisher of computer-related information and the leading global provider of information services on information technology. International Data Group publishes over 235 computer publications in 67 countries. More than fifty million people read one or more International Data Group publications each month. The officers are Patrick J. McGovern, Founder and Board Chairman; Kelly Conlin, President; Jim Casella, Chief Operating Officer. International Data Group's publications include: **ARGENTINA'S** Computerworld Argentina, Infoworld Argentina; **AUSTRALIA'S** Computerworld Australia, Computer Living, Australian PC World, Australian Macworld, Network World, Mobile Business Australia, Publish!, Reseller, IDG Sources; **AUSTRIA'S** Computerwelt Oesterreich, PC Test; **BELGIUM'S** Data News (CW); **BOLIVIA'S** Computerworld; **BRAZIL'S** Computerworld, Connections, Game Power, Mundo Unix, PC World, Publish, Super Game; **BULGARIA'S** Computerworld Bulgaria, PC & Mac World Bulgaria, Network World Bulgaria; **CANADA'S** CIO Canada, Computerworld Canada, InfoCanada, Network World Canada, Reseller; **CHILE'S** Computerworld Chile, Informatica; **COLOMBIA'S** Computerworld Colombia, PC World; **COSTA RICA'S** PC World; **CZECH REPUBLIC'S** Computerworld, Elektronika, PC World; **DENMARK'S** Communications World, Computerworld Danmark, Computerworld Focus, Macintosh Produktkatalog, Macworld Danmark, PC World Danmark, PC Produktguide, Tech World, Windows World; **ECUADOR'S** PC World Ecuador; **EGYPT'S** Computerworld (CW) Middle East, PC World Middle East; **FINLAND'S** MikroPC, Tietoviikko, Tietoverkko; **FRANCE'S** Distributique, GOLDEN MAC, InfoPC, Le Guide du Monde Informatique, Le Monde Informatique, Telecoms & Reseaux; **GERMANY'S** Computerwoche, Computerwoche Focus, Computerwoche Extra, Electronic Entertainment, Gamepro, Information Management, Macwelt, Netzwelt, PC Welt, Publish, Publish; **GREECE'S** Publish & Macworld; **HONG KONG'S** Computerworld Hong Kong, PC World Hong Kong; **HUNGARY'S** Computerworld SZT, PC World; **INDIA'S** Computers & Communications; **INDONESIA'S** Info Komputer; **IRELAND'S** ComputerScope; **ISRAEL'S** Beyond Windows, Computerworld Israel, Multimedia, PC World Israel; **ITALY'S** Computerworld Italia, Lotus Magazine, Macworld Italia, Networking Italia, PC Shopping Italy, PC World Italia; **JAPAN'S** Computerworld Today, Information Systems World, Macworld Japan, Nikkei Personal Computing, SunWorld Japan, Windows World; **KENYA'S** East African Computer News; **KOREA'S** Computerworld Korea, Macworld Korea, PC World Korea; **LATIN AMERICA'S** GamePro; **MALAYSIA'S** Computerworld Malaysia, PC World Malaysia; **MEXICO'S** Compu Edicion, Compu Manufactura, Computacion/Punto de Venta, Computerworld Mexico, MacWorld, Mundo Unix, PC World, Windows; **THE NETHERLANDS'** Computer! Totaal, Computable (CW), LAN Magazine, Lotus Magazine, MacWorld; **NEW ZEALAND'S** Computer Buyer, Computerworld New Zealand, Network World, New Zealand PC World; **NIGERIA'S** PC World Africa; **NORWAY'S** Computerworld Norge, Lotusworld Norge, Macworld Norge, Maxi Data, Networld, PC World Ekspress, PC World Nettverk, PC World Norge, PC World's Produktguide, Publish& Multimedia World, Student Data, Unix World, Windowsworld; **PAKISTAN'S** PC World Pakistan; **PANAMA'S** PC World Panama; **PERU'S** Computerworld Peru, PC World; **PEOPLE'S REPUBLIC OF CHINA'S** China Computerworld, China Infoworld, China PC Info Magazine, Computer Fan, PC World China, Electronics International, Electronics Today/Multimedia World, Electronic Product World, China Network World, Software World Magazine, Telecom Product World; **PHILIPPINES'** Computerworld Philippines, PC Digest (PCW); **POLAND'S** Computerworld Poland, Computerworld Special Report, Networld, PC World/Komputer, Sunworld; **PORTUGAL'S** Cerebro/PC World, Correio Informatico/Computerworld, MacIn; **ROMANIA'S** Computerworld, PC World, Telecom Romania; **RUSSIA'S** Computerworld-Moscow, Mir - PK (PCW), Sety (Networks); **SINGAPORE'S** Computerworld Southeast Asia, PC World Singapore; **SLOVENIA'S** Monitor Magazine; **SOUTH AFRICA'S** Computer Mail (CIO),Computing S.A.,Network World S.A., Software World; **SPAIN'S** Advanced Systems, Amiga World, Computerworld Espana, Communicaciones World, Macworld Espana, NeXTWORLD, Super Juegos Magazine (GamePro), PC World Espana, Publish; **SWEDEN'S** Attack, ComputerSweden, Corporate Computing, Macworld, Mikrodatorn, Natverk & Kommunikation, PC World, CAP & Design, Datalngenjoren, Maxi Data,Windows World; **SWITZERLAND'S** Computerworld Schweiz, Macworld Schweiz, PC Tip; **TAIWAN'S** Computerworld Taiwan, PC World Taiwan; **THAILAND'S** Thai Computerworld; **TURKEY'S** Computerworld Monitor, Macworld Turkiye, PC World Turkiye; **UKRAINE'S** Computerworld, Computers+Software Magazine; **UNITED KINGDOM'S** Computing /Computerworld, Connexion/Network World, Lotus Magazine, Macworld, Open Computing/Sunworld; **UNITED STATES'** Advanced Systems, AmigaWorld, Cable in the Classroom, CD Review, CIO, Computerworld, Computerworld Client/Server Journal, Digital Video, DOS World, Electronic Entertainment Magazine (E2), Federal Computer Week, Game Hits, GamePro, IDG Books, Infoworld, Laser Event, Macworld, Maximize, Multimedia World, Network World, PC Letter, PC World, Publish, SWATPro, Video Event; **URUGUAY'S** PC World Uruguay; **VENEZUELA'S** Computerworld Venezuela, PC World; **VIETNAM'S** PC World Vietnam.

For More Information...

For general information on IDG Books in the U.S., including information on discounts and premiums, contact IDG Books at 800-434-3422.

For information on where to purchase IDG's books outside the U.S., contact Christina Turner at 415-655-3022.

For information on translations, contact Marc Jeffrey Mikulich, Foreign Rights Manager, at IDG Books Worldwide; fax number: 415-655-3295.

For sales inquiries and special prices for bulk quantities, contact Tony Real at 800-434-3422 or 415-655-3048.

For information on using IDG's books in the classroom and ordering examination copies, contact Jim Kelly at 800-434-2086.

Internet World books are distributed in Canada by Macmillan of Canada, a Division of Canada Publishing Corporation; by Computer and Technical Books in Miami, Florida, for South America and the Caribbean; by Longman Singapore in Singapore, Malaysia, Thailand, and Korea; by Toppan Co. Ltd. in Japan; by Asia Computerworld in Hong Kong; by Woodslane Pty. Ltd. in Australia and New Zealand; and by McGraw-Hill Book Company (Europe) Ltd. in the U.K., Europe, the Middle East and Africa.

From Internet World Books

With INTERNET WORLD books, the first name in Internet magazine publishing and the first name in Internet book publishing now join together to bring you an exciting new series of easy-to-use handbooks and guides written and edited by the finest Internet writers working today.

Building upon the success of *Internet World* magazine and in close cooperation with its staff of writers, researchers, and Net practitioners, INTERNET WORLD books offer a full panoply of Net-oriented resources—from beginner guides to volumes targeted to business professionals, Internet publishers, corporate network administrators, and web site developers, as well as to professional researchers, librarians, and home Internet users at all levels.

These books are written with care and intelligence, with accuracy and authority, by the foremost experts in their fields. In addition, the bundling of potent connectivity and search software with selected titles in the series will broaden their inherent usefulness and provide immediate access to the vast fluid contents of the Internet itself.

One key element illuminates all of these features—their focus on the needs of the reader. Each book in this series is user-friendly, in the great tradition of IDG Books, and each is intended to bring the reader toward proficiency and authority in using the Internet to its fullest as a complement to all the other ways the reader creates, gathers, processes, and distributes information.

The scope of INTERNET WORLD books is to serve you as Internet user, whether you are a dedicated "nethead" or a novice sitting down to your first session on the Net. Whatever your level, INTERNET WORLD books are designed to fulfill your need. Beyond this, the series will evolve to meet the demands of an increasingly literate and sophisticated Net audience, presenting new and dynamic ways of using the Internet within the context of our business and personal lives.

Alan M. Meckler	Christopher J. Williams
Chairman and C.E.O.	Group Publisher and V.P.
Mecklermedia Corporation	IDG Books Worldwide, Inc.

Credits

IDG Books Worldwide, Inc.

Group Publisher and V.P.
Christopher J. Williams

Publishing Director
John Osborn

Acquisitions Manager
Amorette Pedersen

Editorial Director
Anne Marie Walker

Production Director
Beth A. Roberts

Manuscript Editor
Carol Henry

Design and Illustration
Benchmark Productions

Composition and Layout
Benchmark Productions

CD Production
Open Text Corporation

Mecklermedia Corporation

Publisher
Tony Abbott

Managing Editor
Carol Davidson

Copyeditor
John Harmon

Proofreader
Angela Miccinello

Dedication

To Noah and Indigo—may they someday make use of all this.

Acknowledgments

I wrote this, but a lot of people's influences are in it. And there are others who may not have contributed to the book, but have contributed to me.

First of all, there are my parents, without whom (if my biology serves me) this would not have been possible. They bought me my first computer (a Timex-Sinclair with a whopping 16K of memory) put me through college—old-fashioned but true—and gave me a place to stay for too many years. Thanks. And thanks to Don and Fran, my brother and sister, for all sorts of things from showing me (unsuccessfully) how to throw a curve ball, to telling me what makes a good résumé.

Brian Cutler and Kelly Hoffman (neé Kreiger) got me started on Albany State's Vax 8650, and that's where my Net experience began. Spencine Hendricks and Denise Gilgannon were two terrific bosses who put up with my fiddling on the office's computers, rather than writing the press releases or taking the photos I was supposed to. Dianne McDonald gave me a job at *PC Magazine* to add some legitimacy to my rantings, and then Gail Shaffer brought me over to the networking side of things. Daniel Dern bought my first article for *Internet World*, bad as it was. But an in's an in. And Michael "Spartacus" Neubarth had enough faith to rescue me from *PC Mag* and Ziff-Davis and bring me over to IW once I knew what I was talking about. Thanks, all.

Then there's Eric Berlin, my best friend and *IW* co-columnist. He keeps me in line, and comes up with a lot of good ideas. Kirsten "Super Nurse" Asmus wins the title of World's Best Girlfriend for putting up with me through a lot of this process. There are plenty of others: Jenny Zimmer, Tommy Noble, Simona Nass, Andy Needleman, and a lot of the Mecklermedia and *Internet World* people: Tanya, Tristan, Jeremy, Suzy, and more. Friends are good to have.

Enough of this. You're here to learn about the Internet. Go to it, and I'll see you on the Net.

Foreword

When Andrew Kantor and I began working at *Internet World* magazine almost two years ago, we received phone calls every day asking, "What is the Internet?" and "Can you tell me how to join the Internet?" We received so many calls that our company set up a 900 number to provide basic Internet information.

We saw an obvious need for a good basic primer that would help people quickly and easily understand what the Internet was and how to be part of it. When we surveyed the available literature, we could find no single book that was to our liking. Meanwhile, Andrew began writing the Entry Level columns for *Internet World* and giving Internet basics seminars at our *Internet World* trade shows and other events. Out of these sources grew the kernel of this book. The core chapters offer plain and precise descriptions of Internet applications and straightforward directions for using them. By following this guide, you should be able to connect to the Internet and become adept at basic navigation in short order.

It is a good time to be getting on the Internet. There are more access providers, better navigation programs, and more useful information and resources than ever before. Moreover, the number of new Internet members and ventures continues to increase dramatically from one month to the next.

In its 26-year history, the Internet has grown from four computers in California and Nevada to more than 5 million registered computer "hosts" worldwide. The number of people who regularly use the Internet is estimated between 20 and 30 million.

Over the last few years the Internet has skyrocketed into prominence and has become a major cultural, business, political, and social medium. Almost every company, organization, university, and government agency is on the Internet, and millions of individuals log on daily from their homes. For people throughout the world, the Internet has become a cultural, business, and educational arena that can no longer be ignored.

You'll find that there's something for everyone on the Internet, from serious professional research and business discourse to hobby forums and games. The Net is a haven for sports fans, movie buffs, pet lovers, science-fiction fanatics, recipe hounds, and, of course, computer geeks. The Internet community has been characterized by the generous nature of its citizens in giving their time and energy to providing services and content and offering helpful advice.

Along with the Internet's rise have come new tools and interfaces. A few years ago, navigating the Internet typically required typing Unix text commands. Today, a host of graphical programs allows users to fetch files, read mail, and surf colorful World-Wide Web sites simply by pointing and clicking. But the older Net still pervades the new, and a basic knowledge of Unix and traditional applications (Archie, FTP, Gopher, Telnet, *et al.*) is necessary to fully comprehend and use the Internet. This guide will give you that basic knowledge and point you to further sources.

These pages can also serve as a path to *Internet World* readership. When you have mastered its lessons, you'll be ready for an ongoing Internet guide and information source. You'll soon graduate from Internet "newbie" status and will yearn for more hearty fare. Some Internet publications are ongoing beginners guides, but serving basic "How to Use the Internet" information issue after issue becomes tedious and ultimately useless to you once you know the ropes.

Thus, we have positioned *Internet World* as a more sophisticated guide and a higher-level source of Internet information. We do provide entry-level columns to bring new people into the Internet community and get them up to speed, and this book will further that cause. But once you know how to get around, you'll appreciate ongoing Internet news coverage and learning more about the issues and personalities that drive the Net.

The Internet continues to grow and change. There are so many new and exciting sites and services, and the resources and content continue to get richer. There are also a host of complex issues that must be addressed—such as censorship, copyright, libel, encryption, and digital transactions. As you look for guidance in your cyberspace travels, Andrew and I and the rest of the *Internet World* staff will be there to continue to enlighten and serve you. See you on the Net!

Michael Neubarth
Editor-in-Chief
Internet World

Contents

Preface xviii

Part One: Getting Started 1

Chapter 1: What is the Internet? 3
This Is the Internet 4

Chapter 2: Getting on the Internet 7
Types of Internet Access 7
   Shell Accounts 7
   SLIP and PPP Access 8
   Specialized Software 11
Finding Internet Access Providers 11
   Other Ways to Find Providers 13
   The Big Guns 14
   Local or National? 15
Picking a Provider 15
Internet Costs 17

Chapter 3: Unix Basics 21
Unix Commands 22
The Pico Editor 24
Important Unix Files 25
   profile or .cshrc 26
   signature 27
   .plan 28
Telnet 29

Contents

Part Two: Using the Internet 31

Chapter 4: Electronic Mail 33

Using E-mail 35
    Pine 36
    Elm 37
    Sending Mail with Elm 38
    Eudora, et al 39
Sending Binary Files 41
Using Mailing Lists 42
E-mail Netiquette 43
Some Interesting Mailing Lists 45
Surfer's Diary: E-mail Address Book 50

Chapter 5: Usenet News 53

What Is Usenet News? 53
    Subscribing to Newsgroups 56
    Setting Up a Graphical Newsreader 58
Reading News 58
    The nn Newsreader 59
    The trn Newsreader 61
    Commands for Using nn and trn 63
    Sending Messages with nn and trn 63
    Using Graphical Newsreaders 64
    Binary Postings 65
Usenet Netiquette 66
Some Usenet Newsgroups to Try 68
    Usenet Newsgroups 69

Chapter 6: Internet Relay Chat (IRC) ...71

Using IRC 72

xiv

Contents

    General IRC Commands 74
        Graphical IRC 77

Chapter 7: Anonymous ftp and Archie .79
    Using FTP 80
        FTP by E-mail 83
        Dot What? 84
    Good FTP Sites 85
        WUArchive 85
        CICA 85
        Sumex-Aim 85
        The Internet Society .86
        RTFM 86
    All About Archie 86
    Surfer's Diary: Interesting and
        Useful FTP Sites 90

Chapter 8: Gopher and Veronica 93
    Gopher Is Your Guide 94
    Using Gopher 95
        Gopher Via a Web Browser 97
    Good Gopher Sites 97
    Surfer's Diary: Interesting and
        Useful Gopher Sites .99

Chapter 9: The World-Wide Web 101
    Using the Web 104
    Using a Text Browser .105
        The Line-Mode Browser 105
        Lynx 106

Contents

    Using a Graphical Browser 108
        All-in-One 110
    Good Web Sites 112
    Surfer's Diary: Interesting and
        Useful Web Pages 118

Part 3: Moving Ahead 121

Chapter 10: Getting Good 123
    E-Mail 123
    Usenet News 124
    IRC 125
    Gopher 126
    The World-Wide Web 126

Chapter 11: Gaining Perspective 129
    Common Misconceptions 130
        Isn't the Internet run by the government? . . .130
        Isn't the Internet a large computer
            near Alexandria, Virginia? 131
        Don't pornographic images
            make up most of the Internet? 131
        Isn't it illegal to advertise on the Internet? . .132
        Isn't it unsafe to send my credit card
            number over the Net? 133
        Isn't e-mail free? 135
        Isn't it a long-distance call to get
            information from Sweden? 135
        Aren't viruses a problem?
            Can't you get one from e-mail? 136

Doesn't everyone hate newbies
   on the Internet? 137
Isn't there a directory of everyone's
   address on the Internet? 137
If you can get files from other computers,
   can other people get into your
   hard drive? 138
A Day in the Life 138

Chapter 12: Useful Resources 143

A Final Note 145

Glossary 147

Appendix: Guide to
Included Software 157

Index 167

Preface

There are a lot of books about the Internet. That's telling—it is no longer just a hot topic or this month's media darling. For millions of people, the Internet has become an everyday thing. It is a tool they use.

That's an important way of looking at the Net: not as a frightening, giant, multinational computer network, but as a tool—a way to communicate with people and to find the information you need. We don't think of toasters as coils of red-hot wires connected to a rheostat; it's how we toast our bread. We don't think of as CD player as a sophisticated microprocessor connected to an unimaginably narrow laser; it's how we play our music. In the same way, the Internet isn't a what anymore. It's a how. It's how we write to friends and family, or check the weather, or get pictures to look at, or do medical research.

But that doesn't make it easy to use. This book may.

"Less is more" was my friend Jill Wohl's motto back in high school, and that's often the case. I set out to write a book that would get people started on the Internet without being a daunting 300- or 400-page volume. When a beginners' book weighs more than a good steak dinner, something's wrong.

Don't get me wrong—I could go on about the Internet for pages and pages. But, here I've tried to trim the fat, to write a streamlined primer that will get you started and set you on your way. This isn't supposed to be the be-all and end-all Internet guide . . . just the be-all and end-all beginner's book.

—Andrew Kantor
ak@iw.com, ak@panix.com

part one

getting started

*a*ll right, enough talk. It's time to do the Net. There are millions of people and billions of files and terabytes of information awaiting you out there. In order to get to them, you need to get on the Internet. You've already taken the first step by buying this book. The next step is to get a good understanding about what the Internet is (if you think it's a giant online service, you're wrong). Once you have that in mind, you can get yourself online and get started.

So let's.

CHAPTER ONE

what is the Internet?

he Internet isn't a thing; it's a lot of things—about 5 million computers connected around the world. Those computers are at colleges and universities, government offices, and corporations and other organizations all over the globe. They weren't connected by accident, and they weren't connected overnight. Like all good stories, this one begins with...

Once upon a time, the Russians were not our friends. The U.S. government, ever paranoid that our Slavic rivals would bomb us back to the Stone Age, decided to come up with a way for our scientists, researchers, and military people to communicate even if much of the country were a smoldering ruin.

Getting Started

Those people were already using computers—big, hulking mainframe machines, but computers nevertheless. And the government wanted them to be able to share information easily. So the Advanced Research Projects Agency (ARPA) decided to connect or *network* those machines. In 1969, they did: Four computers, three in California and one in Utah, were wired together into what was christened the *ARPAnet*.

What was the big deal about connecting computers? Besides the wiring that was required, the experts had to make sure the networked computers could communicate over a distance—that if one computer spoke, the others would listen. But the real beauty of the ARPAnet was its use of *packet switching*. This new technology was designed to connect computers so that messages would get transferred in the best possible way.

Packet *What?*

Packet switching is the bomb-proof technology that makes the Internet work.

Think of the Postal Service. If you want to send a letter from New York to Los Angeles, you don't write on the envelope, "Take this to Columbus, then Chicago, then Des Moines, then San Francisco, then Los Angeles." You just let the Postal Service figure out how to get it to Los Angeles. So if Chicago has been flooded or there's a blackout in San Francisco, your letter will still get through.

That's how packet switching works. If one of those four ARPAnet computers isn't working (either because the Soviets nuked it or a

Chapter 1: What Is the Internet?

> farmer dug too deep one day and cut a power line), the others can still share information; it would just be routed around the disabled computer.
>
> Does it work for sure? You bet; during the Gulf War the Allied military was unable to knock out the Iraqi military network because it used—you guessed it—packet-switching technology.

The ARPAnet and packet switching were a success, so much so that other organizations started using the same technology to network their own computers. Throughout the 1970s and into the 1980s, computer networks based on the ARPAnet's technology began to spring up around the country. Multicampus universities connected their computers. Research groups did the same. Soon there were dozens, then hundreds of computer networks. And then, in the late 1970s, those networks started to connect to one another using the ARPAnet (which itself had been expanding across the country) as the core.

A group of computers is called a *network*. A group of networks is called an *internetwork*. And thus the Internet was born.

That's the short version of the story.

Today the Internet is composed of about 4 to 6 million computers around the world. There are over 25 million people working for the various organizations that own

Getting Started

those computers, and about 10 to 15 million of them use the Internet in some way on a regular basis.

This Is the Internet

Don't think of the Internet as a single thing. It isn't. Think of it as a lot of computers at a lot of organizations. IBM has computers on the Internet. So does the U.S. government. So do colleges and universities. So do individuals. And, just as you decide what to put on your home computer, each organization with a computer connected to the Net is responsible for what they make available to the rest of the Net. No one owns the Internet, but everyone owns a piece of it.

That means the information you get from any of those computers could be right or wrong, current or outdated, interesting or offensive, unique or duplicated. In short, you can find anything on the Internet. That's good and bad. Good because you're likely to find the answer to any question you can ask, *somewhere*. Bad because you can't be sure the answer is right—unless you're sure of the source. (You can probably trust Toyota's information about Corolla prices, but can you trust Jake's Internet Auto Shop?) The Internet is like a flea market of computers.

And because no one owns or runs the Internet, there are no official rules to follow. No one government's laws control the Internet, and no organization can tell any other what it can and cannot make available. After all, it's your computer, and you can do what you like with it.

Despite the questionable nature of some of the information available on the Net, it remains an incredibly useful resource—and why not? With 5 million computers full of information, there's bound to be something good for everyone.

So why is everyone so excited about the Internet? What do they do on it? Two things, basically: They communicate and they trade information. That's it. But it's a lot, as you'll soon see. There are different ways to use the Internet to communicate, and different ways to find information. But first you have to be *connected*.

CHAPTER TWO

getting on the Internet

getting on the Internet used to be difficult to do—few companies provided connections, and the software was tough to use. But things have changed, and although it isn't quite a matter of clicking your heels together three times, getting on the Net is a pretty straightforward task. This chapter gives you the basics.

Keep in mind that the Internet is not a service. It's just a collection of a few million computers that happen to be connected. There is no 1-800-INTERNET number to call for an account, and there is no technical support line. You are, essentially, on your own. You have to do two things: Buy the right software and find someone to connect you.

Getting Started

> **Getting on the Net**
> You need all of these:
> - Computer (PC or Mac)
> - Modem
> - Communications software (either general or Internet-specific)
> - An Internet access provider—someone who will connect you

If you want access to the Internet, all you have to do is get connected to one of its 5 million or so computers. Some of those computers are at corporations and other organizations (maybe even your own), and some belong to companies whose sole purpose is to provide access to the Internet for individuals. These are called *Internet access providers*.

Getting on the Internet might be easier than you think. Most colleges and many corporations are already part of the Internet. If you are at a college or university, there's a good chance you can get free Net access through the school's computer system. Ask in the Computer Center, or bug a professor in the CompSci department.

If your company has a local area network (LAN) and offices in other locations, there's a good chance it's connected to the Internet. Of course, that doesn't mean *you* have access, but it may only be a matter of talking to your system administrator about installing some software on your desktop machine. The good part about this kind of connection is that it's fast and easy to use; there's no fancy setup required, and you won't need a modem. You can also use all sorts of graphical Mac and Windows software. Of course, in this case you'll likely be limited to using the connection from the office and not from home.

But if you want to reach the Net from home and you don't work for a connected company—if it's just you and your modem—don't fret. You're in the majority. What you want, then, is *dial-up access*. This means you use your computer and modem to call or "dial up" one of those Internet access providers that is connected to the Internet.

Chapter 2: Getting on the Internet

That provider most likely uses a Unix computer or a group of them, meaning that instead of running DOS or the Macintosh operating system, the provider runs Unix. Unix is a complicated but powerful operating system that is able to run a machine with dozens of simultaneous users, including you.

Before you start looking for an Internet access provider, you should think about *how* you want to connect to the Internet.

Types of Internet Access

If you have a connection to the Internet through your office and don't have to use a modem, you have what is known as a *direct connection*. Consider yourself lucky; you will be able to use a lot of fancy Internet tools that are designed for Windows or the Macintosh.

But if you aren't so blessed, and you have to dial up to another computer with your modem—as anyone who wants to access the Internet from home must do—you have a choice between two types of connections: a *shell account* or a *SLIP connection*. (Not all Internet providers offer both.) See Table 2-1.

Shell Accounts

The most fundamental and most popular type of Internet connection is a shell account. You use your modem to dial

Getting Started

into a more powerful computer, most likely one running the Unix operating system. You are actually controlling that other computer from your home with your keyboard, and seeing its messages on your monitor. Your home computer is hardly doing anything.

With a shell account, everything you see is plain text. There are no fancy graphics, and you won't be able to use your mouse much, if at all. Some providers will give you an easy-to-use menu of Internet services: Press 1 for e-mail, press 2 for FTP, and some other choices that we'll cover later. Many providers won't even do that—you'll have a plain Unix prompt (like a DOS C:> prompt, but probably a dollar or percent sign instead), and you'll have to know the right commands to type. It can be intimidating, but it's not hard to learn.

Shell accounts are usually inexpensive, often costing less than $20 a month. To use the acount, all you need is standard communications software, such as Procomm Plus for DOS or Windows, or ZTerm for the Macintosh. If you're masochistic or low on cash, you can even use the Windows Terminal application. But an investment in a good piece of communications software will pay off quickly.

SLIP and PPP Access

The alternative to a shell account is a SLIP or PPP connection. (PPP is a newer, slightly better version of SLIP, but many people refer to both as a SLIP connection.) To get briefly technical, SLIP stands for serial-line internetworking protocol. A serial line is a telephone line, so SLIP actually means "a way to use the Internet through a phone line." Many local access providers offer SLIP/PPP connections at a slightly higher price than a shell account.

With a shell account, your computer simply controls another computer that is on the Internet. But with a SLIP connection, your computer is actually a *part* of the Internet, as one of the millions that compose it. The Internet provider you dial into isn't doing much work other than passing data to your home computer for processing. There are several advantages and disadvantages to this type of connection.

Chapter 2: Getting on the Internet

With a SLIP connection, you need a special kind of software to dial your provider. You can't use ordinary communications software. Some well-known commercial packages are Internet in a Box, Internet Chameleon, Internet Anywhere for Windows, and Synergy's VersaTerm-Link or InterCon's TCP/Connect II for the Macintosh. There are also plenty of free communications products available on the Internet, but you need to be familiar with file transfer procedures in order to retrieve that software. (We'll go over file transfer in Chapter 7.)

The advantage of a SLIP/PPP connection is that you can use software designed to take advantage of the Windows or Macintosh graphical interface. Instead of typing in commands, you can use your mouse to make selections. There is plenty of good software out there, including a package called Mosaic and one called Netscape. (Many people consider them the "killer applications" of the Internet—they'll be covered in Chapter 9.)

But there are disadvantages to a SLIP connection. The software you need for it is often more expensive than standard communications software that you might already own. SLIP access typically costs more than a simple shell account, too. And because SLIP software is graphical, it doesn't work as fast as standard, text-based software. Much more data must travel over the phone lines to your home computer than with a non-SLIP connection. If you have a slow computer, forget it.

Table 2-1:
Shell Account vs. SLIP/PPP Connection

SHELL	SLIP/PPP
Use any communications software	Need special, more expensive software
Easy to set up—just dial	Setup somewhat more complicated
Cheap ($20 per month on average)	More expensive ($30–$40 per month or more)
Text-based and fast	Graphical but slower

Getting Started

Table 2-1 *Continued*: Shell Account vs. SLIP/PPP Connection

SHELL	SLIP/PPP
Need to know some Unix commands	Use Windows or Mac applications
Must use provider's chosen e-mail, Usenet, Gopher, and other software	Choose your own software—commercial or shareware

Regardless of the provider you use and the type of connection you have, the things you can do on the Internet are the same. That is one of the beauties of the Net: No matter what angle you approach it from, it remains ... the Internet.

Setting Up SLIP

With a shell account, all you need to know is the phone number of your access provider, your username, your password, and, of course, how to use your communications software. With a SLIP/PPP connection, on the other hand, you need to know a bit more.

Any software that makes a SLIP connection needs certain kinds of information that your access provider will supply:

- **Your IP address.** This is your numerical address on the Internet. You'll probably never use it after you set yourself up, but you'll need to know it at least at first. It will be something like **123.45.123.456**. Some providers use *dynamic IP addresses* in which you get a different address each time you connect.

- **Your subnet mask or Netmask.** This is another part of your addressing scheme. It will look like **255.255.255.0**.

- **The nameserver(s).** This is the IP address of the provider's computer that your computer will connect to. It might look a lot like your IP address, but with a different number at the end.

- **Your host name.** This will be your user ID–it will probably be something simple like **kara** or **jsmith**.

- **The provider's domain name.** This is the name of your provider–something like **access.com** or **provider.com**. It might also be something like **ppp.access.com** or **users.provider.com**.

  For your e-mail software, you'll need to know the **POP account** and **SMTP mail server**. The POP account is the full address to which your

> mail will be sent. *It may be longer than your e-mail address.* For instance, if your e-mail address is **ak@provider.com**, your POP account might be **ak@mail.provider.com**. The SMTP server will be the last part of that POP account: **mail.provider.com**.
>
> - **The NNTP news server.** Like the SMTP server, it is the name of the computer that handles Usenet News. It will probably have a name like **news.provider.com** or possibly just **provider.com**.
>
> Good products such as Internet in a Box and Internet Anywhere will explain what each of these numbers is and how to set up the software. A good provider will give you all this information in an easy-to-understand format.

Specialized Software

There is a middle ground between shell accounts and SLIP/PPP connections: providers that offer their own, specialized software *instead* of shell accounts or SLIP connections. Major online services such as America Online and Prodigy will gladly give you their own software free of charge, so you can access their service and then access the Internet. Although this software is typically easy to use, it's the only software you can use with these companies. If you don't like AOL's software, you're stuck unless you switch to another service.

Some Internet access providers offer specialized, proprietary software for use on their systems as an *alternative* to shell accounts and SLIP connections. (Thus they may give you three choices: shell, SLIP/PPP, *or* their own interface.) Unfortunately, even if their own software is wonderful, it is "married" to their service; Netcom's software will only run on Netcom, for instance.

In contrast to both of these, learning some basic Unix commands will allow you to use the Internet with *any* provider. And, as you'll see, the software you use with a SLIP/PPP connection can also be used with any Internet provider that supports SLIP or PPP.

Finding Internet Access Providers

It isn't always easy to find an Internet access provider. Because no one is in charge of the whole Internet, there is

Getting Started

no central list of providers. Several people and organizations have compiled lists, but they aren't always complete, and they are almost definitely out-of-date. But they're all you have to work with.

When looking for an Internet provider, start by asking around; a friend or co-worker might already be accessing the Internet and can recommend a provider nearby. Word-of-mouth is one of the most powerful means of finding out about the Internet.

If that doesn't work, there are lists of Internet providers on the Internet. A major caveat: These lists are not always up-to-date, and they are not always accurate. New providers emerge, coverage changes, and some go out of business. And even the methods described below for finding a provider may no longer work—welcome to the Internet.

Of course, in order to get these lists you need to be on the Internet; it's sort of a catch-22. Find a friend who has access to Internet e-mail—through America Online, CompuServe, or Prodigy, for example, or possibly through her company. She sends a special message to an address on the Internet, and automatically receives the provider information via e-mail. (E-mail is explained in Chapter 4.)

Various organizations maintain lists of access providers, and some are better than others. The best list around (at the time of this writing, anyway) is called, simply, The List. Your e-mail-enabled friend can get it by sending a four-line message to the address **ftpmail@decwrl.dec.com** that reads

```
connect ftp.colossus.net
chdir /
get list
quit
```

An older but better-known list is the PDIAL (Public Dial-up Internet Access List). It isn't updated frequently, however, although a new version is expected to be published by the end of 1995. You can get the PDIAL by having your friend send an e-mail message to **info-deli-server@netcom.com**. The subject line should read `send pdial`; the body of the message can be empty.

In both these cases it can take anywhere from a few hours to a couple of days to get a reply. That reply will be a

Chapter 2: Getting on the Internet

list of Internet providers sorted by name or area code. You can go through the list to find a provider near you, then call and find out if they offer what you want.

What *do* you want? The upcoming section, "Picking a Provider," will help you decide.

Other Ways to Find Providers

Look in the back of books. Many Internet reference books have Internet access provider lists in the back. Although these are likely outdated, they can also provide a starting point for getting access.

Post to Usenet. If you have a friend who is on the Internet, he or she can post a message to Usenet News (see Chapter 3). The newsgroup **alt.internet.access-wanted** is the place for people looking for providers in their area; you—your friend, actually—are likely to find some providers by asking there.

Go with a Big Gun. You can always sign up with one of the large national providers (see "The Big Guns," below). Once you're connected to the Net, even if you aren't paying the best rates, you can always find a better, local provider by retrieving one of the lists I've mentioned, or by posting to Usenet News. Switching providers is not a big deal because they all connect you to the same thing: the Internet.

Finding Access Providers

- Check with your organization (you might already be connected)
- Ask a friend or colleague
- If you have access to e-mail (through a friend or an online service):

    Send a message to **ftpmail@decwrl.dec.com** that reads

    ```
    connect ftp.colossus.net
    chdir /
    get list
    quit
    ```

    Send a message to **info-deli-server@netcom.com** with a subject line of **send pdial**.

Getting Started

The Big Guns

Besides the smaller, local Internet access providers, there are large companies offering nationwide Internet access. Three of these companies specialize in Internet access. America Online, CompuServe, Delphi, the Microsoft Network, and Prodigy are *online services* that *also* offer connections to the Internet.

Alternet is one of the largest access providers in the United States, and it offers access for individuals as well as large organizations. Alternet's number is (800) 258-9695.

America Online is an online service that also offers Internet access; it provides its own software. AOL's number is (800) 827-6364.

CompuServe is an online service, but they also offer Internet access through a separate division of the company—you don't need to sign up for the service to access the Internet. CompuServe's phone number is (800) 848-8990.

Delphi offers a text-based menu system, and at least one graphical interface is available. Delphi can be reached at (800) 695-4005.

The Microsoft Network will include its software in the Windows 95 operating environment, scheduled for release by the end of 1995. Microsoft promises that it will offer access to the Internet.

Netcom has local phone numbers around much of the United States and offers its own graphical interface. Netcom's phone number is (800) 501-8649.

Performance Systems International (PSI) started as a corporate access provider and has expanded its services to include individuals. The company also has access numbers nationwide. PSI provides shell accounts, SLIP connections, and its own software as well. You can reach PSI at (800) 774-3031.

Prodigy, like AOL, is an online service that also offers Internet access. The company also provides its own software. Prodigy's phone number is (800) 776-3449.

Local or National?

Should you choose a national provider or a local one? National providers have the advantage of a large, tested organization. But you have to pay for that. Local providers can offer more personal service but are not always as reliable.

How about an online service? They typically charge significantly higher rates than Internet access providers; you're paying for things you may never use—such as the file libraries, chat rooms, and other non-Internet features of the service. Unless you *want* America Online or Prodigy, you're probably better off using a company that specializes in Internet access.

With an online service, you also must use their software; Prodigy customers use Prodigy's interface and America Online customers use that service's. But even with the most basic Internet provider, you have some choice in the interface you use. If you have a SLIP/PPP connection (explained earlier in this chapter), you can choose exactly the software you want. And, especially with a small local provider, you have more say in how things are done—you can ask that they provide certain services, or that they change your username, without having to go through a large bureaucracy.

Lastly, despite the continual influx of online service users, there is a certain stigma on the Internet when people see an address that ends in **aol.com** or **prodigy.com**. This isn't fair, but it's true.

Picking a Provider

Once you've found some providers in your area, you have to pick one. If you're lucky, you live in an area with several to choose from, and market forces will keep the services top-notch. If not, there's still a good chance that a reliable company is offering Internet access in your area. And remember: You can always switch providers at any time, just as you can switch long-distance telephone companies.

When you talk to the people who run the system, make sure they offer 14.4-Kbps access (just call it "fourteen-four

Getting Started

access"). You also want at least e-mail, Usenet News, telnet, and FTP services. What are those things? *Usenet News* is the Internet's bulletin board system where millions of people trade messages on thousands of topics (see Chapter 5). *Telnet* lets you connect from your computer to another for a variety of reasons (see Chapter 3). *FTP* lets you get files of software, research papers, and even song lyrics from computers around the world (see Chapter 7). Most providers offer more, but these are the basics you'll need.

Pricing will differ. Some providers offer a monthly flat rate, some charge by the hour, and some use a combination. Choose what's best for you. If you plan to use the Internet a lot, try to get a flat rate. If you're only planning to check your e-mail and maybe a few Usenet newsgroups each day, an hourly rate may be less expensive.

Also be aware that some providers ask you to pay for a certain amount of time in advance—a month, three months, or even more—especially if they charge a flat rate. There may be a penalty for signing up for a shorter amount of time. And those that charge hourly and bill your credit card may continue to bill you even if you quit, so be sure to check the policy for leaving their service.

What to Ask a Provider

- Do you offer the access I want (shell or SLIP/PPP)?
- How much do you charge for the kind of access I want? Per month? Per hour? Is there a startup cost?

Chapter 2: Getting on the Internet

- If I choose a shell account, what kind of interface or menu do you have?
- What's the highest modem speed you support? Does it cost extra?
- How many modems do you have? How many users? (If the ratio is greater than ten users to a modem, you may be faced with frequent busy signals.)
- Do you offer e-mail, Usenet News, telnet, and FTP? How much disk space on your system can I use for storing files I retrieve from the Net?
- How about built-in Archie, Gopher, and World-Wide Web software—do you have these for shell account users?
- Do you offer technical support? By phone? What hours?

Once you pick a provider, sign up. You'll probably pay by credit card, although many providers accept checks and money orders. They'll give you a *username* and an Internet e-mail address, as well as instructions for logging on. If you aren't familiar with using your modem, it may take a little while to get used to the procedure. But soon enough you'll be logging on without thinking twice.

Tip: If you are completely unfamiliar with your modem and communications software, the easiest thing to do is read the modem and software manuals. There are also plenty of books that will teach you the basics of using these components, including Ziff-Davis Press's *How To Connect* and IDG's *Modems For Dummies*.

Internet Costs

One of the beauties of the Internet is the fact that it is so inexpensive to use. Unlike the telephone system, you aren't charged by how much you use the Net, or where you send messages, or what you do. You pay one rate (flat or hourly) for using the Internet, period. If you take an hour to write one message to someone in the same city, you'll pay the same as if you spend an hour looking at information on a computer in Sweden.

Getting Started

Let's say you pay an Internet access provider $19.95 per month for access. Let's also say that the phone number of this provider is local, so you only pay $0.10 per call. *Those are your only costs for using the Internet.*

You can send a hundred e-mail messages, retrieve dozens of games from computers around the world, engage in 20 conversations with a few hundred people, and do research on six topics, using computers in the U.S., Europe, and Asia. It still only costs you $19.95 per month, plus $0.10 for each time you call your provider. If you call twice a day for a month, your total cost for using the Net is $19.95 + $6.00 or $25.95.

All that for less than thirty bucks. Quite a deal, eh?

Is this figure a good average? You bet. At worst, you'll have to pay per-minute to call your access provider if it's a few towns away. But you never have to pay for what you do once you're online. You don't pay more to send an e-mail message to Japan, and you don't pay more if you follow 20 Usenet newsgroups. (Usenet is covered in Chapter 5.)

CHAPTER THREE

unix basics

nix is a complex, complicated, and powerful operating system. It is also the operating system of choice for most of the Internet. If your access to the Internet is through a shell account, you'll have to know a few Unix commands to get by.

Many users of the Internet already work with Unix. For newcomers, improved and easier-to-use software helps avoid the hassle and headache that Unix can cause. (Although, like owning a '69 Chevy, many people take great pleasure in tinkering with Unix, headaches and all.) But shell accounts are popular, (although they are becoming less so) and many people have only a shell account to work with, so they still deserve coverage.

Getting Started

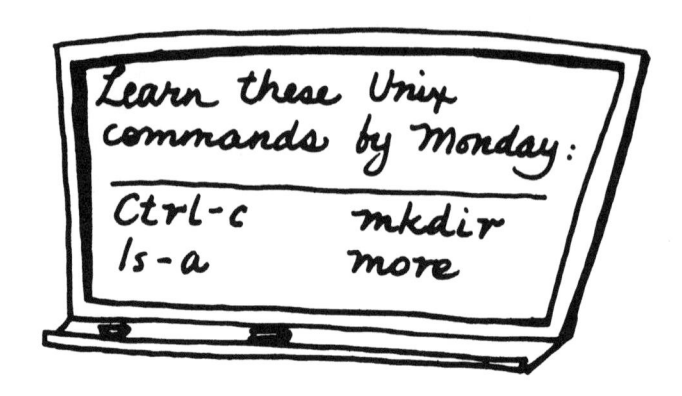

Unix Commands

Unix uses a command line, as DOS does. (There are graphical versions of Unix as well, but you won't see them with a shell account.) The Unix prompt is often a dollar sign or a percent sign, and sometimes something more complex, like /users/andrew>.

With a shell account, remember—you are using a Unix system. Like a DOS computer's directories or a Mac's folders, files on a Unix system are also arranged in directories. As a user, you have a personal area: your *home directory*. You will use it to store certain files Unix needs (more on that in a moment), as well as any files you retrieve from the Internet. Each system will be different, but most commands are the same from machine to machine.

Here in Table 3-1 are the most important commands to know. (In this table, "Ctrl-*x*" means hold down the <Ctrl> key and press the key for the letter represented by the *x*.)

Table 3-1: Basic Unix Comands

Command	Description
Ctrl-c	Interrupt or cancel whatever you're doing.
Ctrl-l	Redisplay the screen—useful when things get messy.

Table 3-1 Continued:
Basic Unix Comands

Command	Description
ls, ls -a	List the contents in your current directory, much like DOS's **dir** command. Using **ls -a** lists hidden command-like files such as .newsrc.
man *topic*	Provide the help (manual) file for a particular topic. Entering **man archie** at the prompt gives you the manual page for the archie command, for instance. You can also use the > to redirect that information to a file. If you enter **man archie > archie.txt** you get a file called archie.txt that contains the entire manual entry. You can then download that file (see **sz**, **sx**) and view it at your leisure.
cp *file*	Makes an identical copy of the specified *file* (like DOS's **copy**).
mv *filename* *newname*	Rename a file or move it to another directory, like DOS's **ren** or **move**. Using the command **mv *filename newname*** gives a file a new name, but keeps it in the same directory. Using **mv *filename /newdirectory*** keeps the name, but moves it to another directory on the computer.
rm *filename*	Delete a file. Unlike DOS and the Mac, however, "rm is forever." Once you remove a file, it is virtually impossible to undelete or recover it without, at best, causing your system administrator a lot of grief.
sz *filename*, sx *filename*	Send a file from the Unix computer to your desktop PC using either the Zmodem or Xmodem protocol. Once you use the command **sz *filename*,** you must tell your PC to receive the file. However, most software will start receiving Zmodem transfers automatically.

Getting Started

Table 3-1 *Continued*: Basic Unix Comands

Command	Description
rz *filename*, rx *filename*	Receive a file from your desktop PC using the Zmodem or Xmodem protocols. After you give the rz command, you must tell your PC to begin sending the file.
more	Display a (text) file one screen at a time. Useful for viewing long documents.
mkdir	Create a subdirectory of the current directory. If you are in the /users/andrew directory and give the **mkdir docs** command, it will create a directory /users/andrew/docs.

The Pico Editor

Like DOS Edit, Windows Notepad, and Mac Teachtext, Unix has several built-in text editors. If you're using a shell account, you'll need to be familiar with at least one of them.

Many Unix gurus swear by the venerable **vi** editor because it's powerful and—once you get familiar with it—

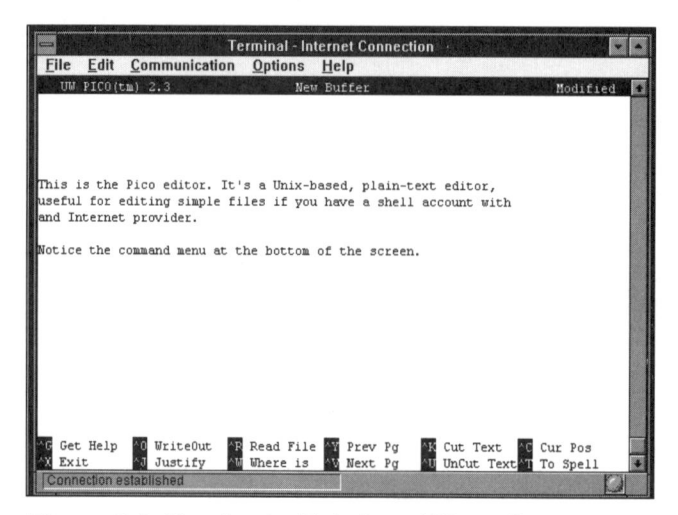

Figure 3-1 The simple, Unix-based Pico editor.

24

quick to use. But vi requires you to remember some odd commands (**<esc>** : **w** to save a file, for instance). Pico, on the other hand (see Figure 3-1), is an easier-to-use editor that will do everything you need.

You start Pico by entering **pico** at the Unix prompt (or, if your provider has a menu, by selecting the appropriate item—something like "Pico editor" or "Edit files"). To edit a text file that already exists, enter **pico** *filename* instead, as in **pico .signature**.

The Pico screen will pop up. On the bottom is a menu of commands (see Table 3-2), and that's one of the nice things about this editor. If you're creating a new file, the screen will be blank and you can start typing away. If you've chosen to edit an existing file, that file will appear on the screen.

Table 3-2: Basic Pico Commands

COMMAND	DESCRIPTION
Ctrl-O	Save the file you're working on
Ctrl-K	Delete the current line
Ctrl-U	Undelete everything you've just deleted with Ctrl-K
Ctrl-R	Insert a file into the text
Ctrl-W	Find text ("**W**here is . . . ?")
Ctrl-G	Get help
Ctrl-X	Exit

When you exit with Ctrl-X and have changed the file you're working on, Pico will ask if you want to save the file. Unless you want to lose all your changes, press Y. If you were editing an existing file, Pico will then make sure you want to use the same filename; just press the <Enter> key. Eventually, you'll get used to the save and exit keystrokes: Ctrl-X, Y, <Enter>.

Important Unix Files

With a Unix shell account, you get space on that Unix machine. It's called your directory or your *home directory*, and it works just like a directory on a PC or a folder on a

Getting Started

Mac. It's a space for you to store your files and sort of a home base from which you'll access the Internet.

The files in your directory are whatever you put there. If you use FTP to retrieve a game, for instance (see Chapter 7), it will reside in your directory until you download it to your PC. If you save e-mail messages, they will also remain in your directory.

Unix uses some important files that may or may not be in your home directory already. (A good provider will make sure they are.) If those files are there, you may want to use Pico to edit them. If they aren't, you'll want to create them to make it easier to get around the Internet.

.profile or .cshrc

If you're a PC user, you're probably familiar with the autoexec.bat file, a simple text file that contains a list of instructions your computer carries out automatically when you start it. Unix systems work the same way. A file called **.profile** or **.cshrc** contains a list of commands that set up your account to behave properly...and can make things easier for you.

Why either .profile *or* .cshrc? Unix systems have several slightly different interfaces called *shells*. Although the major commands are the same in every one, there are certain differences. The shells have names such as *sh* (the Bourne shell), *csh* (C shell, pronounced "seashell"), and *ksh* (the Korn shell). You can ask your provider which shell you have. The Bourne and Korn shells use .profile; the C shell uses .cshrc.

Both these files are similar and contain lines that look like this:

```
alias lam telnet lambda.parc.xerox.com:8888
alias f finger
alias panix telnet panix.com
alias rtfm ftp rtfm.mit.edu
EDITOR=/usr/local/bin/pico
export EDITOR
NAME="Andrew Kantor"
export NAME
```

Tip: If you want to have as little to do with Unix as possible, just remember the most important lines in your .profile or .cshrc are alias lines and the EDITOR line.

Chapter 3: Unix Basics

An alias line allows you to type in a simple letter or phrase in place of a longer, more complicated command. That's useful for complex commands you use often. The alias line contains the word **alias**, then the abbreviation you want to use, then the command you want to abbreviate. In the example above, we have aliased **lam** so that entering it executes the command

```
telnet lambda.parc.xerox.com:8888
```

(You'll read about telnet in the next section). That's a lot easier than typing that whole command! If you use a certain procedure a lot, you should create an alias for it in your .profile or .cshrc file to speed things up.

The **EDITOR** and **export EDITOR** lines tell the computer that anytime it wants you to edit a file—when you're writing a post for Usenet News or sending an e-mail message—it will default to Pico instead of to vi or a more complicated Unix editor. If you don't use the EDITOR command, you might suddenly find yourself in a program you aren't familiar with. EDITOR helps keep things simple.

.signature

When you send an electronic mail message or post an article to Usenet News (you'll learn about these in Chapters 4 and 5, respectively), you can have a short message automatically attached to the end of your note, like a signature at the end of a letter you write. Whatever you put in your **.signature** file (called your "sig" or your "dot sig") will go in that attachment.

Getting Started

A basic .signature might look like this:

```
-------------------------------------------------
John Smith              "There ain't no such thing
jsmith@bigcorp.com       as a free lunch."
-------------------------------------------------
```

Many people put a disclaimer in their .sig ("This does not necessarily reflect the opinion of my company"), and some people create long, complex .sigs. Because of that, some Internet providers limit the length of a user's .sig to four lines.

To create a signature, simply use the Pico command: **pico .signature**. Write what you want, keeping in mind that it will automatically end up at the end of *every* message you write (see Figure 3-2). Save the file in your Unix home directory and that's it. You can change or remove your .signature any time you want, as often as you want.

If you have a SLIP/PPP or direct connection to the Internet, most e-mail and Usenet News software will have a menu choice for at least one signature file.

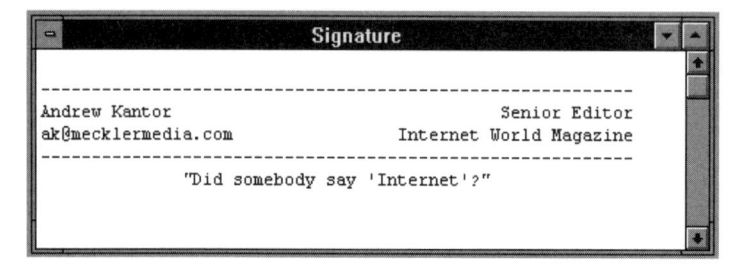

```
---------------------------------------------------------
Andrew Kantor                                Senior Editor
ak@mecklermedia.com               Internet World Magazine
---------------------------------------------------------
              "Did somebody say 'Internet'?"
```

Figure 3-2 Your signature file is one way to express your individuality or just tell people who you are.

.plan

Other users on the Internet can find out if you maintain a pre-packaged bit of information. It's called a **.plan** file. Like your .signature, it resides on the Unix computer you use, in your home directory. Your .plan can be as long as you want. It will automatically show your username, real name, the

Chapter 3: Unix Basics

last time you logged in, and some other information about you—plus whatever you have added to your .plan file.

How would someone see it? By using the **finger** command. For instance, if you enter **finger ak@mecklermedia.com** at your Unix prompt, you'll see my .plan.

Here's an example that assumes you have a standard Unix dollar-sign prompt:

```
$ finger jsmith@bigcorp.com

[bigcorp.com]
Login name: jsmith  In real life: John Smith
Directory: /users/j/jsmith  Shell: /usr/local/bin/ksh
Last login Fri Aug 8 15:41 on ttyp2 from comp.bigcorp.com
Plan:
I'm John Smith, director of marketing for the Big
Corporation. You can reach me during the day at
(203) 958-2427.
```

> **Tip:** If you're interested in becoming a Unix guru–or just learning the more esoteric and powerful commands–O'Reilly & Associates's *Unix in a Nutshell* is a terrific reference.

Telnet

Telnet is one of the simplest tools on the Internet, but also one of the most useful. Simply put, telnet allows you to connect and log on to another computer on the Internet. Many computers have been set up to allow visitors to log on and search for information or even play games.

More importantly, the telnet command can allow you to use Internet tools that aren't available on your local provider's machine. For instance, later we'll cover Archie, which lets you search the Internet for files and software. Some Internet providers don't have Archie available, but you can use the telnet command to reach a computer that does. From there you can run your search. There are many public machines set up for similar situations, and you can

Getting Started

use Archie, Gopher, and even access the World Wide Web from these computers. (More on those in later chapters.)

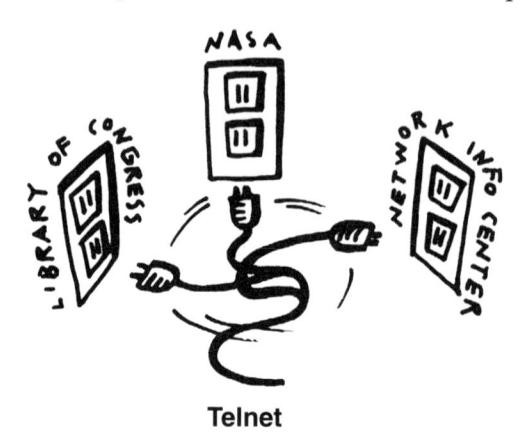

Telnet

Telnet is also useful if you have an account on a computer in one part of the world and you happen to be in another—a college student on summer vacation, for instance. If you have access to the Net from wherever you are, you can telnet to the computer on which you have your account, to check mail and the like.

To use the telnet command, you must know the name of the computer you want to reach. You can find this name by reading an article in a magazine such as *Internet World,* or from someone else on the Internet. Computer names are divided into two or more parts, separated by periods or dots. An example is **locis.loc.gov.** Sometimes telnet addresses have a number at the end, such as 8888. So you might be told to telnet to **public.archie.rutgers.edu 8888**, for instance.

You will also need instructions for what to do once you get to the other computer. Usually, you will be told to use a certain log-in name. It might be *visitor, guest,* or the name of the tool you wish to use, such as *archie.* A few sites do not require any special log-in commands.

Telnet is easy to use, and you may find it allows you to employ Internet tools and navigators you normally wouldn't have access to. When you choose an Internet provider, make sure that telnet is available.

part two

using the internet

you're about to open a toolbox—a collection of utilities that will help you communicate and get information like never before. But a toolbox is useless without some idea of what you can build with it.

The Internet is about communications and information. Once you get started—and believe me, there is some work involved—you'll find you have a whole new world to explore.

You can send electronic mail to friends, colleagues, family, and even strangers around the world. It's as fast as a phone call but as relaxed as a letter in the mail. Communicate with magazine editors, politicians, business people, and millions of others without the formality of a letter (or the wait for it to be delivered). Avoid long-distance phone bills by sending a short e-mail message instead.

Want to share your hobby or profession with someone but can't find a lot of people nearby? The Internet removes

Using the Internet

those outdated geographic boundries. From stamp collectors to exotic-automobile mechanics, skiers to surgeons, you'll find them all on the Net and willing to talk.

See a mistake in last night's *Mad About You?* Read a good book lately? Tell other people about it. Doing research for a report? Need to know the population of Arizona or the lyrics to "American Pie"? There is more information on the Internet than in all the libraries of the world. Want a picture of a caffeine molecule or a guide to buying in-line skates? They're both on the Net. And a lot more.

Think of the Internet as a combination postal service, telephone system, party line, used bookstore, and library. You can write to a particular person or join in a discussion with hundreds of strangers. You can search for a single piece of information or browse through the collective knowledge of a planet.

You're about to start collecting tools. What you build with them is up to you.

CHAPTER FOUR

electronic mail

he most popular means of communicating through the Internet is with electronic mail or *e-mail*. E-mail works a lot like ordinary postal mail. You write a message, address it, and send it on its way. On the other end, the person or people to whom you send it will see that a message from you has arrived and can then read it. E-mail usually takes only a few minutes to get delivered, even if the recipient is on the other side of the globe.

Everyone on the Internet has an e-mail address. Like postal addresses, some are long and complicated, and others are short and sweet. They all have several things in common.

All postal addresses have the person's name, street address, city, state, country, and zip code. Internet addresses work

Using the Internet

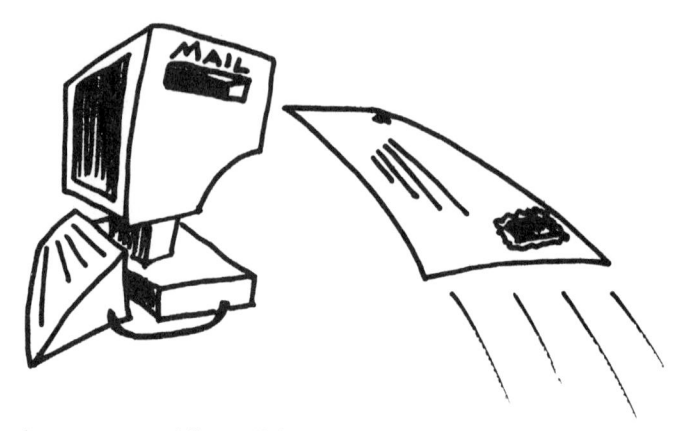

the same way. They all have a user's name, the @ sign, the name of the user's computer, a period, and the type of organization. Commercial organizations have the letters .com at the end; government computers have the letters .gov. Educational sites have the letters .edu. There's also .mil for the military, .org for nonprofit organizations, .uk for British sites, .il for those in Israel, and many others.

An Internet address contains no spaces and is always in lowercase characters. An example of an address is

    akantor@mecklermedia.com

You can reach the President of the U.S. at

    president@whitehouse.gov

Just as a postal address can include an apartment number or company division, some people have longer and more complex Internet addresses. These addresses may contain strange symbols such as percent signs, exclamation points, or words that don't make sense. And not all users' names are their actual names. Some people use their initials, and others will use their first initial and last name. John Smith might use john, or smith, or js, or jsmith.

School or organization names can also be long, especially if they include the name of the department or even the individual computer. A company's e-mail address might be

    jsmith%marketing@foobar.pittsburgh.ibm.com

or even longer than that. If someone gives you their e-mail address, trust it—no matter how strange or cryptic it seems.

Chapter 4: Electronic Mail

There are many different e-mail programs available. If you have a standard Unix shell account, you may be able to choose from programs called Mail, Elm, and Pine. If you have a SLIP account or a direct line from your office, you may have a program called Eudora.

No matter what software you use, the basics of using e-mail are the same.

Every message has at least one recipient, and most messages have a subject line. After that comes the body of the message. When you create a message, you tell your mail program to whom the mail is going, then write a short subject, then write your message. When you finish, you give the Send command used by your software. In a short time, your message will reach the recipient, who will be notified by a message that says "You have new mail."

Using E-mail

Just as there are many different word processors (WordPerfect, Microsoft Word, Ami Pro, and the like) there are many different programs for sending, receiving, and organizing electronic mail. On Unix systems, two of the most popular—and best, especially for newcomers—are *Pine* and *Elm*. For users with a SLIP/PPP or direct connection, Qualcomm's Eudora (either the freeware or the commercial version) is arguably the best around, but there are

Using the Internet

several others, including Spry's Air Mail and a freeware package called Pegasus.

All e-mail programs work pretty much the same way. You start them, and they check for any new mail waiting for you. You can then write a new letter or read the messages waiting for you. Most programs support "folders," which help you better organize your messages. If you're working on a project involving frogs, for instance, you can create a Frogs folder to hold all related messages for easy retrieval.

Pine

On a Unix shell account, you start Pine by either entering **pine** at the prompt or selecting it from a menu, if one is offered. If it's your first time using Pine, the program will ask if you want it to create the directories it needs. Answer Yes. From then on, your opening screen will look like Figure 4-1.

Pine automatically checks your mail when you start; you'll see a message such as

    [Folder "INBOX" opened with 6 messages]

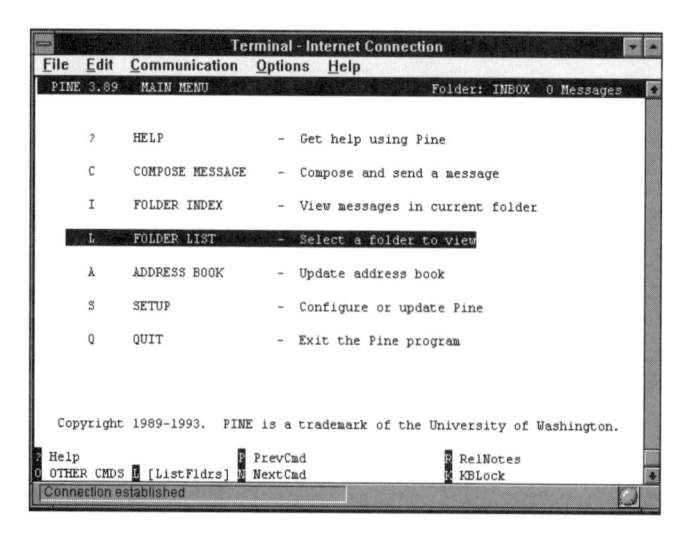

Figure 4-1 The text-based Pine e-mail program lets you choose options from a menu.

Chapter 4: Electronic Mail

Pine starts you off on its Main Menu; you can usually get back to it by pressing M at any other menu. From the Main Menu, to read your mail:

1. Select Folder List (with your arrow keys or by pressing **L**).
2. Select your Inbox—it will be the first folder on the list.
3. Pine will show you all your new messages.
4. Using the arrow keys, select a message and press <Enter> to open it.

Once you've finished reading a message, you can reply to it, forward it to someone else, discard it, or store it in a folder to keep it organized (see Table 4-1).

Pine also supports an address book. With it, you can assign nicknames to people you write to frequently. Rather than entering **kara@baxter.com**, for instance, you can simply send a message to **kara**. To use the address book, just select A from the Main Menu, and press A again to add a name.

Elm

Elm (Figure 4-2) starts much like Pine.

1. From the prompt, enter **elm** (or select it from the menu, depending on your system).
2. Answer **Yes** at the prompt to create a subdirectory.
3. You are now at the main screen: the Inbox.

Elm provides an easy way to remember commands; as with Pine, they're at the bottom of the screen. You can use the arrow keys (or the j and k keys, if your arrows don't work) to move from message to message. Pressing <Enter> will let you read the selected message; from there you can delete it, reply, forward it, or put it in a folder (see Table 4-1).

In addition, when you first start Elm, it creates a hidden directory called .elm. You can go into it by using the **cd** command (**cd .elm**). You'll find a file called elmrc that you can edit with Pico (**pico elmrc**). The elmrc file is fairly self-explanatory and is used to set all sorts of user options, such as what questions Elm asks you when you quit, and whether to automatically save outgoing messages in a Sent folder.

Using the Internet

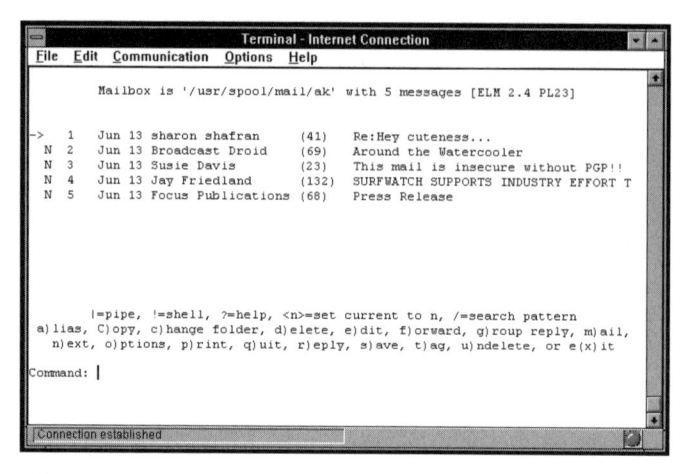

```
                    Terminal - Internet Connection
 File  Edit  Communication  Options  Help

        Mailbox is '/usr/spool/mail/ak' with 5 messages [ELM 2.4 PL23]

->  1   Jun 13 sharon shafran      (41)   Re:Hey cuteness...
    N 2 Jun 13 Broadcast Droid     (69)   Around the Watercooler
    N 3 Jun 13 Susie Davis         (23)   This mail is insecure without PGP!!
    N 4 Jun 13 Jay Friedland       (132)  SURFWATCH SUPPORTS INDUSTRY EFFORT T
    N 5 Jun 13 Focus Publications  (68)   Press Release




         |=pipe, !=shell, ?=help, <n>=set current to n, /=search pattern
 a)lias, C)opy, c)hange folder, d)elete, e)dit, f)orward, g)roup reply, m)ail,
    n)ext, o)ptions, p)rint, q)uit, r)eply, s)ave, t)ag, u)ndelete, or e(x)it
Command: |


Connection established
```

Figure 4-2 Elm is another popular e-mail program among shell account users.

Elm supports an address book for frequently used addresses. You can get to it by pressing **a** from any mailbox and then pressing n to add a new entry or "alias." From a mailbox you can also press o for a list of options, including what Elm will use as an editor (it should read something like /usr/local/bin/pico). You don't have to worry about the other settings.

Sending Mail with Elm

When you want to send a message in Elm (either a new letter or one you're forwarding), you'll be using the Pico editor. When you're finished writing, press Ctrl-X. Elm responds with the cryptic

```
Save modified buffer (ANSWERING "No" WILL
DESTROY CHANGES) (y/n)?
```

Translation: Is the message OK? Chances are you'll answer Yes by pressing Y.

Elm then responds with something like

```
File Name to write: /tmp/snd.10005.
```

Chapter 4: Electronic Mail

Don't worry about this; Elm is creating a temporary file before it sends your mail, and for some reason the programmer wanted you to know about it. Just press <Enter>.

Table 4-1: Using Pine and Elm

ACTION	PINE	ELM
Read new mail	Select Folder List, then Inbox	Opens Inbox automatically
Create new message	c	m
Reply to message	r	r
Forward message	f	f
Delete message	d	d
Store in a folder	s	s
Open a different folder	l	c
Get help	?	?
Quit	q	x

Note: *Pine also lets you cancel what you're doing—sending, etc.—by pressing Ctrl-C. With Elm you can often do this by pressing <Enter> at a prompt without entering any information.*

Eudora, et al

If you have a SLIP connection to the Internet or can reach the Net through your office, you can use a graphical e-mail package such as Eudora, a freeware program from Qualcomm for both Windows and the Macintosh (see Figure 4-3). Qualcomm also makes a more full-featured commercial version. It's an excellent piece of software that makes using e-mail a pleasure. And if you're using a suite of Internet access programs like Internet in a Box or Internet Anywhere, it probably comes with its own graphical e-mail software.

Graphical e-mail software often requires you to give it some information—basically, the name of the computer from which you will be getting e-mail. Your Internet access provider should give you this; it includes your POP account (similar or identical to your e-mail address) and your SMTP server (the name of the computer handling your e-mail). If

Using the Internet

your provider is provider.com, for instance, your SMTP server is probably something like mail.provider.com.

As with any Windows or Mac application, you start Eudora (or whatever software you're using) by double-clicking on the icon. Most packages start by showing you your inbox of received mail.

You can then double-click on individual messages to read them. Like Pine and Elm, Eudora and other graphical e-mail programs let you reply to messages, forward them, store them in folders, and delete them using either menu commands or by clicking on the appropriate toolbar icon.

To create a new message, you choose New Message from the menu or the toolbar, fill in the addressee(s), the subject, and the message itself or *body*. Click on the Send button and it's away, arriving at its destination usually within minutes.

Most if not all graphical e-mail programs, including Eudora, have an address book; Eudora calls these addresses "nicknames." Just as with the Unix e-mail software, you can use the address book to keep the nicknames of the people you write to often, again using **kara** instead of **kara@baxter.com**, for instance.

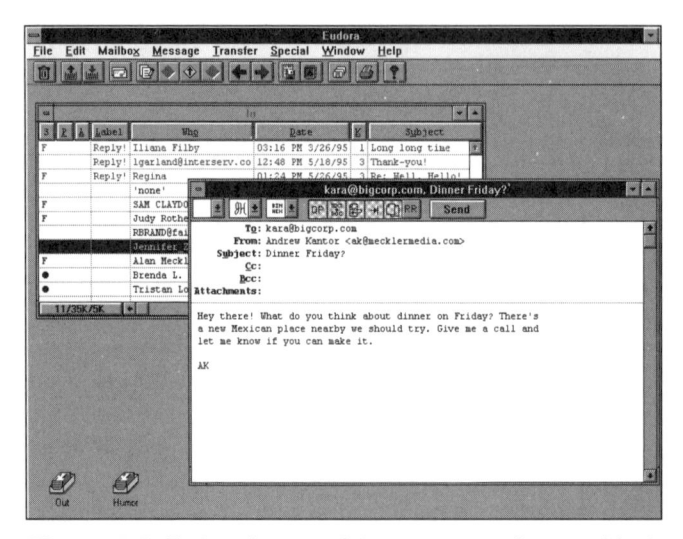

Figure 4-3 Eudora is one of the most popular graphical e-mail products.

Chapter 4: Electronic Mail

> **Getting Eudora**
> A freeware version of Eudora is available on the Net. You need to use FTP to get it (FTP is covered in Chapter 7). Go to **ftp.qualcomm.com** and look in the **/quest** directory. You'll find directories for both the Windows and Macintosh versions. Version 1 is the freeware program, and the version 2 directory contains add-ons and bug fixes for the commercial version.

Sending Binary Files

Pine, along with most graphical e-mail packages, lets you send binary files (software, graphics, spreadsheets, and the like). These files are called *attachments*. (Commercial online services like CompuServe and Prodigy allow you to send attachments to other members of the same service, but not to anyone else; this is another drawback of using one of these services as an Internet access provider.)

The most popular way of sending an attachment is via a process called *MIME encoding*. MIME stands for Multipurpose Internet Mail Extensions, and it has become the standard for sending nontext files. It sounds complicated, but it's simple from the user's standpoint. You simply address a message normally, write a note to the recipient, and then use your mail software's **attach** command to send the binary file along with your comment. The recipient will get your message along with a note to the effect that there is a binary file attached; the file can then be decoded (if that isn't done automatically).

If you're using Pine, sending a binary file is a simple two-step process. First, you must upload the file from your PC to your shell account using Unix's **rz** command. Once the file resides there, you simply start Pine, create a new message, and press Ctrl-J to attach a file. (Pressing Ctrl-T after Ctrl-J will give you a list of available files.)

When you receive an attachment with Pine, the message will have a + next to it. When you open the message (by selecting it and pressing <Enter>), you will be told that there is an attached file. Pine will tell you that it "Can not display this part. Use the 'V' command to save in a file."

Using the Internet

When you press **V**, you will first have to choose the attachment (Pine considers it part 2 of the message—the text is part 1) and then indicate the name you wish to give it. It is then saved in your shell account directory; use Unix's **sz** command to download it to your PC.

Elm does not support sending binary attachments, but it does allow you to receive them. When you receive an attachment and open the message, Elm will ask you if you want to see the file (it will display as lines of jibberish), write it to a file, or forget it. When you press **2** to write it to a file, you can choose the filename and then download it to your PC.

With a graphical program such as Eudora, sending binary files is as simple as choosing Attach Document or Attach File from a menu. Eudora allows you to choose from among three formats for attaching files: MIME, BinHex, and UUencoding. Because most packages support MIME, that is usually the best way to send it, although certain Macintosh e-mail packages only support BinHex attachments.

Binary files received via a graphical product are usually converted automatically. When you open a message with an attachment in Eudora, for instance, you'll see a message like

    Attachment Converted: C:\TEMP\picture.GIF.

That tells you where the file resides on your hard disk.

Using Mailing Lists

Most people use electronic mail to communicate with one or two people at a time. But with a mailing list, which is sometimes called a *discussion list* or a *listserv,* you can get into ongoing electronic discussions with hundreds of people around the world. Mailing lists are good for people who don't have full Internet access but can send and receive Internet e-mail. That includes customers of CompuServe, Prodigy, or MCI Mail. Joining a mailing list means that one letter can instantly reach thousands of people, and you can share your thoughts with all of them.

Of course, you will receive e-mail messages from all those subscribers, too. Many people who sign up for mailing lists

Chapter 4: Electronic Mail

find that they can't handle the hundreds of messages they receive every day.

You can get a list of Internet mailing lists by e-mail. Send a message to the Internet address **mail-server@rtfm.mit.edu**. The message doesn't need a subject, but the body of it must read

```
send /usenet/news.answers/mail/mailing-
lists/*
```

Be sure to include the asterisk at the end.

You will soon receive several large files that make up the list of mailing lists. The list includes a description of each mailing list and instructions for subscribing. In most cases, you subscribe by sending an e-mail message to a special address—it will probably have a name like **listserv, listproc,** or **majordomo**. Sometimes you will have to send a note to someone and ask to be added to the mailing list.

Once you have joined a mailing list, you'll begin receiving mail from others who have joined. At first it will be confusing; the subscribers will be engaged in conversations that started before you joined. But soon enough you'll be able to follow along, get involved in discussions, and learn all sorts of information from the other participants.

For a sampling of some of the mailing lists you can join, look at the end of this chapter.

E-mail Netiquette

There are certain unwritten rules for behavior on the Internet. Collectively, they're known as *netiquette*, and e-mail has its own rules.

Using the Internet

Quote back messages. Whether in a private message or on a mailing list, when you reply to someone's message you should include their original statements. No one likes getting mail that reads simply, "Good idea!" Most e-mail programs will automatically insert the original text, usually preceding each line with an angle bracket:

```
> What do you think about meeting at the
> ball field around noon? We can carpool
> from there.
```

You can then add your comment underneath, making it easier for people to follow the conversation:

```
> What do you think about meeting at the
> ball field around noon? We can carpool
> from there.

Better make it 12:30. I have some errands
to run in the morning.
```

Send subscription requests to the right place. One of the most frequent complaints of mailing-list subscribers is that people try to unsubscribe from the list by sending a message to the participants of the list, rather than to the administrator. Generally, if you want to send a note to other subscribers, send it to **listname@listserv.somewhere.com**, as in

```
gardening-list@listserv.clark.net
```

If you want to subscribe or unsubscribe from the list, you send it to **listserv@somewhere.com**, as in

```
listserv@listserv.clark.net
```

or some similar name.

Stick to the topic. If you're subscribing to a gardening list, keep messages on the topic of gardening. Of course, some discussions will drift from the topic and that's all right. Just don't *start* one off-topic. People interested in gardening don't necessarily want to hear about your poison ivy experience, even if *you* think there's a connection.

Chapter 4: Electronic Mail

Don't advertise. People who subscribe to a mailing list do not want unsolicited advertisements, on-topic or not. You're likely to get angry e-mail, a note sent to your access provider, or worse, in response.

Some Interesting Mailing Lists

There are thousands of electronic mailing lists available. Some are participatory (you can write to them) and others are receive-only, like David Letterman's Top-Ten list. Here's a sample of 25 mailing lists, including how to subscribe. (Remember, they're free!)

(Note: These lists are active as of the time we went to press. But the Net is ever changing, so there's no guarantee they'll still be there, or that the addresses will still be correct.)

Adoptees: A list for adult adoptees to discuss various aspects of adoption; not intended for nonadoptees.

Send e-mail to:	**adoptees-request@ucsd.edu**
Subject:	\<not required\>
Body:	**subscribe \<Your e-mail address\> adoptees**

Analytic Philosophy: A list for the discussion of analytic philosophy—from history to application.

Send e-mail to:	**analytic-request@cs.brown.edu**
Subject:	**subscribe**
Body:	\<not required\>

Arachnid: For discussions of spiders, scorpions, and other eight-legged creepies.

Send e-mail to:	**majordomo@bga.com**
Subject:	\<not required\>
Body (2 lines):	**subscribe arachnid** **end**

Using the Internet

Ballroom: For discussing all aspects of ballroom and swing dancing, including technique, events, etc.

Send e-mail to:	**listserv@mitvma.mit.edu**
Subject:	<not required>
Body:	**subscribe ballroom <Your Name>**

Barbershop: For discussions of barbershop quartet and other such music.

Send e-mail to: **david.bowen@cray.com**
Politely request to be added to the list.

Biblio: Discussions of fine-book collecting; for collectors, dealers, etc.

Send e-mail to:	**biblio-request@iris.claremont.edu**
Subject:	**subscribe**
Body:	<not required>

Coins: For discussing all topics related to coin and money collecting.

Send e-mail to:	**coins-request@uni.edu**
Subject:	<not required>
Body:	**subscribe coins**

Dinosaur: For scientific discussions of dinosaurs and their kin.

Send e-mail to:	**listproc@lepomis.psych.upenn.edu**
Subject:	<not required>
Body:	**subscribe dinosaur <Your Name>**

Chapter 4: Electronic Mail

Down Syndrome: Discussion and support of Down Syndrome; for parents, relatives, teachers, etc.

Send e-mail to: **listserv@vm1.nodak.edu**
Subject: <not required>
Body: **subscribe down-syn <Your Name>**

Ferrets: For discussing ferrets as animals and as pets.

Send e-mail to: **ferret-request@cunyvm.cuny.edu**
Subject: **subscribe**
Body: <not required>

Fruit-of-the-Day: A silly list that tells you what the official fruit of the day is, every day.

Send e-mail to: **fotd-request@cs.umd.edu**
Subject: **subscribe**
Body: <not required>

Fungus: Dedicated to growing mushrooms.

Send e-mail to: **fungus-request@teleport.com**
Subject: <not required>
Body: **subscribe fungus <Your e-mail address>**

Job-List: Lists of entry-level jobs for recent college grads.

Send e-mail to: **listserv@sun.cc.westga.edu**
Subject: <not required>
Body: **subscribe job-list <Your Name>**

Kids: A mailing list for kids to talk to kids.

Send e-mail to: **kids-request@vms.cis.pitt.edu**
Politely request to be added to the list.

Using the Internet

LuckyTown: For discussing Bruce Springsteen's music.

Send e-mail to:	**luckytown-request@netcom.com**
Subject:	<not required>
Body:	**subscribe luckytown**

Mayberry: Discussions of old Andy Griffith shows such as *The Andy Griffith Show* and *Mayberry RFD*.

Send e-mail to:	**listserv@bolis.sf-bay.org**
Subject:	<not required>
Body:	**subscribe mayberry**

Net-Happenings: Lists of new sites on the Internet (an excellent resource).

Send e-mail to:	**majordomo@is.internic.net**
Subject:	<not required>
Body:	**subscribe net-happenings**

Objectivism: For discussing the philosophy of Ayn Rand.

Send e-mail to: **objectivism-request@vix.com**
Politely request to be added to the list.

Quanta: Discussions about the monthly electronic science-fiction magazine.

Send e-mail to: **da1n@andrew.cmu.edu**
Politely request to be added to the list.

Roots-L: A large and popular genealogy discussion list.

Send e-mail to:	**listserv@vm1.nodak.edu**
Subject:	<not required>
Body:	**sub roots-l <Your Name>**

Skeptic: A list for discussing—and debunking—extraordinary claims of parapsychology, psychics, etc.

Send e-mail to: **listserv@jhuvm.hcf.jhu.edu**
Subject: <not required>
Body: **subscribe skeptic <Your Name>**

Tango: For discussing the Argentine Tango dance, music, and events.

Send e-mail to: **listserv@mitvma.mit.edu**
Subject: <not required>
Body: **subscribe tango <Your Name>**

TopTen: David Letterman's nightly top-ten list, sent daily.

Send e-mail to: **listserv@listserv@clark.net**
Subject: <not required>
Body: **subscribe topten <Your Name>**

Waterski: For discussing the sport, for beginners or experts.

Send e-mail to: **waterski-request@nda.com**
Politely request to be added to the list.

What's On Tonite?: A daily television listing (four editions).

Send e-mail to: **circulation@paperboy.com**
Subject: <not required>
Body: **subscribe <edition> <Your Name>**
Edition is eastern, central, mountain, or pacific.

Surfer's Diary: E-mail Address Book

Name	Address
Bill Clinton	president@whitehouse.gov
Microsoft Info	info@microsoft.com

Surfer's Diary: E-mail Address Book

Name	Address

CHAPTER FIVE

usenet news

e-mail is great for communicating one-to-one, or even one-to-several. But for ongoing discussions with a whole lot of people, there is *Usenet News*.

Technically, Usenet News is not a part of the Internet, but rather uses the Internet as a means of transmission. But the line between Internet and Usenet has become increasingly blurred, and few people bother to make the distinction anymore.

What Is Usenet News?

Usenet News is the electronic bulletin board of the Internet. Think of it as a giant corkboard in a supermarket. Anyone in the town can use a piece of paper and a thumbtack to put a message up—*post* it—for anyone to see (anyone who looks, that is).

Using the Internet

Imagine this big public corkboard is divided into sections: Cars for Sale, Roommate Wanted, and Town Elections. When you tack up a message, you put it in the appropriate section. Throughout the day, other people come by and read your messages. They can also tack up their own message, either in reply to yours or on a different topic.

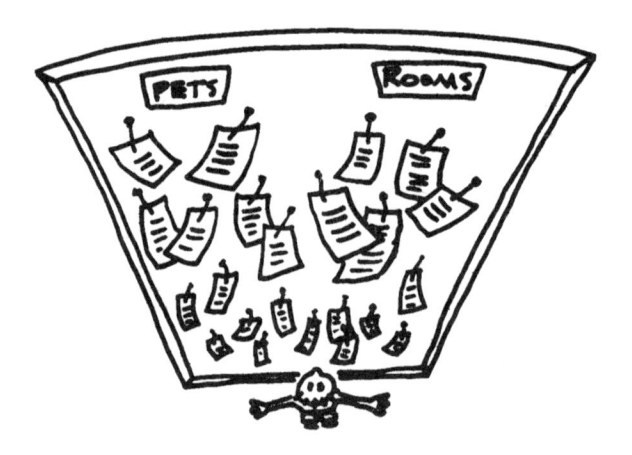

Usenet News works the same way. Its sections are called *newsgroups*. At last count, over 11,000 public newsgroups existed around the world—like having that supermarket board divided into 11,000 sections! They cover every topic imaginable, from children's television to politics, from cars to sex, from music to skiing, and everything in between.

Newsgroups are divided into topics or *hierarchies*. The eight largest or most-widespread of these are: **alt, comp, misc, news, rec, sci, soc,** and **talk**. There are many minor topics, as well, such as **biz** (business) and **clari** (ClariNet, which offers Associated Press and other news for a fee), and newsgroups for geographic areas such as **fj** (Japan), **nyc** (New York City), **ba** (San Francisco Bay Area) and more. Many purists do not consider the alt. hierarchy to be one of the "big eight" because—although it is the largest group—it is less widely distributed than the others.

Chapter 5: Usenet News

Newsgroup names start with the hierarchy abbreviation and then explain the subject they cover. Examples are

```
alt.college.tunnels
rec.arts.tv.sf.babylon5
soc.culture.romania
```

Just as you use e-mail software to send and receive electronic mail, you use special software to read messages on Usenet News. It's called *newsreader* software, and there are several popular programs (more on them in a moment). Essentially, you tell your newsreader software, that you want to read the messages in a certain newsgroup. The software checks to see what's there, then presents you with a list of new messages in that group. You pick the ones that look interesting, read them, and decide if you want to post your own message in reply. It's the equivalent of walking to the town square and seeing if anything new has been tacked up in the Cars for Sale section of the corkboard.

If you want to post your own message, you tell your newsreader that you want to place a note in a particular newsgroup. Your software will prompt you or leave space for the name of the group, the subject, whether you want it to go out to the whole world or just locally, and more. (Some newsgroups are *moderated*, meaning that you can't simply post to them; you send your post to a moderator who decides if it's appropriate.)

Once sent, your message makes its way to the rest of the Internet, where it waits for other people to read and possibly answer.

Getting Started with Usenet

1. Subscribe to newsgroups that interest you by editing your newsrc file.
2. Start your newsreader.
3. From each newsgroup, choose the articles that sound interesting.
4. Read them.
5. If you want to, follow up publicly in Usenet or reply via e-mail.
6. Post a message from scratch.

Using the Internet

Subscribing to Newsgroups

The first thing to do with Usenet is pick some newsgroups that you'll want to follow every day. That's called *subscribing*. If you're a bicycle rider, for instance, you may want to subscribe to **rec.bicycling**. If you're into medicine, there are several **sci.med** groups. When you subscribe, your newsreader will automatically check those groups for new messages every time you ask it to.

To see what newsgroups are available, get a list of them. With a SLIP/PPP or direct connection and a graphical newsreader, you will probably see a box with that list on your screen; it contains all the available newsgroups. In Spry's newsreader, for instance, you choose Newsgroup Browser from a menu and then wait for it to get the list of available newsgroups. Other programs have menu choices such as Show All Newsgroups, with another box showing groups to which you have subscribed. You can drag newsgroup names from one box to the other to subscribe and unsubscribe. Easy! (The first time you use a graphical newsreader, it may take a few minutes for your PC to retrieve the list of all available newsgroups from the Internet.)

With a shell account, there is a file called your **newsrc** file (pronounced "news-are-see") that resides in your home directory as **.newsrc**. (The dot before the name means it's a hidden command file and you need to use Unix's **ls -a** command to see it. See Chapter 3.) The newsrc is a plain text file that lists all the newsgroups your Internet provider has available. Most commercial providers carry almost all the newsgroups, including some that only apply to your local area, so the newsrc can be several thousand lines long. A section of it might look like this:

```
rec.arts.books!
rec.arts.books.marketplace!
rec.arts.books.reviews!
rec.arts.books.tolkien!
rec.arts.cinema!
rec.arts.comics: 1-6435
rec.arts.comics.creative!
rec.arts.comics.marketplace!
```

Chapter 5: Usenet News

```
rec.arts.comics.misc: 1-536
rec.arts.comics.strips!
rec.arts.comics.xbooks!
rec.arts.dance!
rec.arts.disney!
rec.arts.drwho: 1-29753
rec.arts.erotica!
rec.arts.fine!
rec.arts.marching.band.college!
```

An exclamation point (or "bang" in Unix parlance) after a newsgroup name means you have not subscribed to that group. A colon indicates that you have. The numbers indicate which postings to that group you have read. You will need to edit your .newsrc file so your newsreader knows which newsgroups you're interested in. You can, of course, unsubscribe from any group if you get tired of it, or resubscribe after that. Although you don't have to pay for subscribing to a lot of groups, trying to follow too many can be overwhelming.

If you are using a shell account, you will have to edit your .newsrc file manually, using Pico. First, start a newsreader (see next section) to ensure that the .newsrc file is created. For example, you can enter **trn** at the Unix prompt, wait while it does its stuff, then press **q** when it stops. Keep pressing **q** until you're back at the Unix prompt. Presto—you have your own .newsrc file.

Now that you're sure the file exists, use Pico to edit it (see Figure 5-1). Scroll down through the file and, if you see a newsgroup you want to follow, change the exclamation point at the end to a colon and remove any numbers. If you want to subscribe to **rec.humor.funny**, for example, change it from this:

```
rec.humor.funny! 1-3746
```

to this:

```
rec.humor.funny: 1
```

Repeat this with any newsgroups you like. When you're done, exit Pico (using Ctrl-X) and tell it to save the file.

Using the Internet

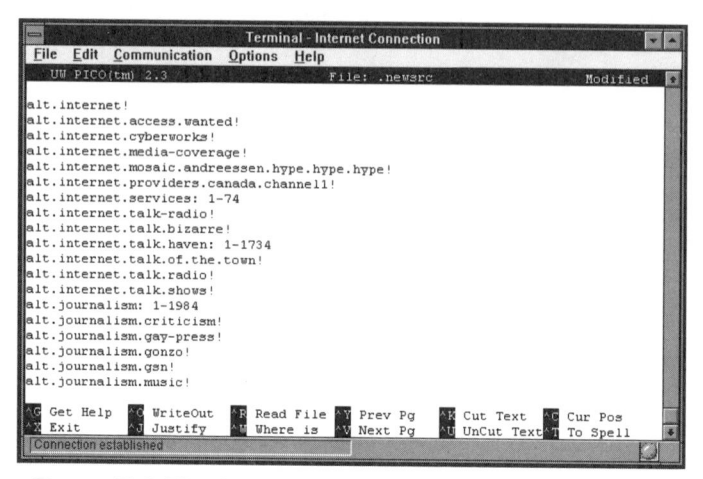

Figure 5-1 Pico is the easiest way to edit your .newsrc file.

Note: Keep in mind that some very active groups may have hundreds of new messages each day, so subscribing to a lot of groups at first may be overwhelming. Pick five or six to start; you can always add more.

Setting Up a Graphical Newsreader

If you're using a graphical newsreader—there are several for PCs as well as Macintoshes—you will have to tell the software the name of the computer that will be providing you with News. That's your *news server* or *NNTP server*, and your Internet provider will tell you the name. It will likely be something like **news.provider.com**.

You are now ready to read Usenet News.

Reading News

If you have a direct or SLIP connection, you can simply double-click on your newsreader's icon to start reading Usenet News. Your software will then get the list of new postings in each group, and you can select the ones you want to read.

With a shell account, however, you will use a text-based Unix newsreader instead. The most popular ones are **rn**

Chapter 5: Usenet News

(read news), **nn** (no news is good news), **trn** (threaded rn), and **tin**. Of those, nn and trn are the best—rn is relatively old and has been replaced by trn; tin remains less stable than the others. Most access providers offer nn, trn, or both.

To start your newsreader, enter its name at the prompt: **nn** or **trn**. Table 5-1 lists common commands used in these two newsreaders.

The newsreader will first check out your .newsrc file to see what groups you've subscribed to and then prepare you to read the messages in the groups you've selected. See Figure 5-2.

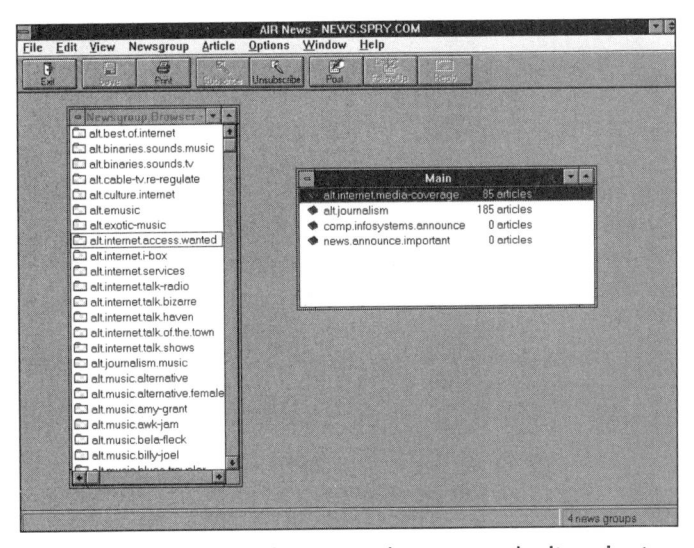

Figure 5-2 Graphical newsreaders can make it easier to sort through and read posts to Usenet newsgroups.

The nn Newsreader

After nn reads your .newsrc file to see which groups you have subscribed to, it automatically shows you the list of unread articles in the first of those groups. These articles are lettered from *a* through *s*, and—depending on the number of unread articles—there may be several screens of articles, each lettered the same way (see Figure 5-3). Next to the letter is the name of the poster, then the size of the message, then the subject. If an article is the first post in a topic, you

Using the Internet

```
┌─────────────────── Telnet - panix.com ───────────────────┐
│ Connect  Edit  Terminal  Help                             │
│ Newsgroup: alt.home.repair          Articles: 275 of 275/1│
│ a root                28  >Squeaky Hinges                 │
│ b Donovan White       19  >>                              │
│ c Ted Swirsky          8  >VCR question <help request!>   │
│ d Steve Ito           16  >                               │
│ e S M Goldwasser      86  >                               │
│ f David Peritt         8  exterior window malding replacement│
│ g John F. Woods       26  >>>>>First Septic Tank Seepage - Help!│
│ h K R VanLuvanee      25  >>>                             │
│ i bsar                 5  hardwood floor maintenance      │
│ j Rick S P840          2  Posting Test                    │
│ k Rick S P840         14  Garage Door and Opener Recommendations Wanted│
│ l Steve Rogovich      41  >                               │
│ m S S Ensminger       18  mixed oak floor                 │
│ n Lance Smith          9  >                               │
│ o ari l. ben          44  >                               │
│ p Coralie J. Allen    13  >HARDWOOD FLOORS * on vacation *│
│ q J.D. Baldwin        17  What do you pay for PMI?        │
│ r David Rumsey        37  >                               │
│ s Rob Pinelli P180    31  >>                              │
│                                                           │
│ -- 15:11 -- SELECT -- help:? ------41%-----               │
└───────────────────────────────────────────────────────────┘
```

Figure 5-3 My favorite Unix newsreader is nn, because it makes it easy to wade through the articles in each group and choose which ones to read.

only see the subject, but if it's a *follow-up* (a response to a message), it will follow the original post and the subject will consist only of at least one angle bracket. So you might see:

```
f John Smith    17   How do I use the Gizmo 2000?
g Jane Doe       6   >
h Bill Johnson   9   >
i Jane Doe      12   >>
j John Smith     9   >>>
```

This indicates a conversation in progress, starting with John Smith's original question.

As you look through the list of articles posted, you select the ones you want to read by pressing the corresponding lowercase letter. When you're finished with one screen, press the Spacebar to go to the next page. If you're on the last page, nn will either show you the articles you've selected, or prompt you to move to the next newsgroup by asking "Junk seen articles?" That's nn's way of asking "Is it OK to mark all these articles as read and move on?" Press the Spacebar or the y to say Yes. If you press n instead, nn will mark those messages as unread, so next time you check out the newsgroup they, will still be there.

> **Tip:** Using a Unix newsreader? Do you want to go back to old messages in a newsgroup? Go to your .newsrc file and find the line for that group. The numbers indicate the messages you've read; if you change "1-2427" to "1-2" you'll have up to 2,425 old messages to read—useful if you want to check out something you saw a few days ago.

The trn Newsreader

If any new newsgroups have been created, trn may ask if you want to subscribe to them. Then trn tells you the first group with new messages and asks if you want to read it:

```
====== 27 unread articles in rec.bicycles.rides — read now? [+ynq]
```

If you press the Spacebar (or the plus sign), trn will show you the new messages in that newsgroup, lettered from *a* through *z* (Figure 5-4).

You can select the articles you want to read by pressing the appropriate letter. Pressing the Spacebar will bring you to the next page of articles from which you can select. When there are no more articles to list, both trn and nn start showing you the articles you selected. When you're done, they switch to the next newsgroup you've subscribed to.

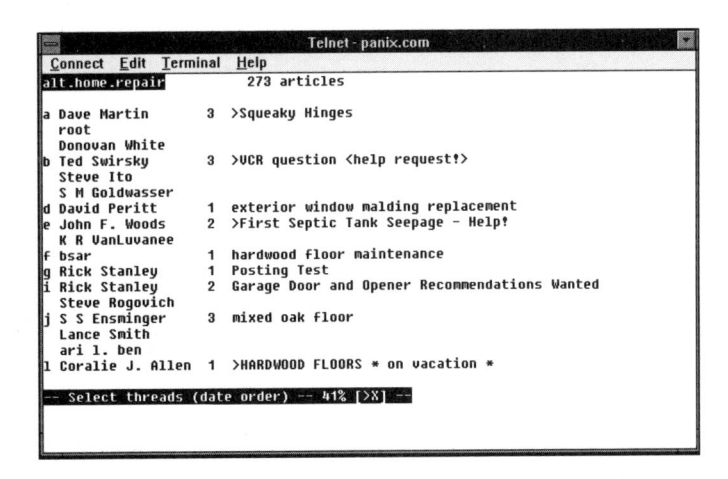

Figure 5-4 The trn newsreader lists new messages in a newsgroup lettered from a through z.

Using the Internet

In fact, pressing the spacebar is what you'll do most of the time—it always selects the default choice, which is usually the one you want.

Table 5.1 is a summary of the commands for nn and trn.

Table 5-1: Commands for Using nn and trn

ACTION	NN	TRN	NOTES
While choosing messages to read:			
Scroll forward through unread articles	<Spacebar>	<Spacebar>	
Scroll backward through unread articles	<	<	
Choose articles to read	<letter>	<letter>	
Go to a specific group	G *newsgroup*	g *newsgroup*	
Choose newsgroup	nn -g, enter name at prompt	trn *newsgroup*	
Go to previous newsgroup	P	P	
While reading messages:			
Read next page of message	<Spacebar>	<Spacebar>	
Read previous page of message	<Backspace>	<	
Read next message	n	n	If you are at the end of an article, <Spacebar> will work
Read previous message	<	-	
UUdecode selected messages	:decode, then a period, then a plus sign	:e, then J	

62

Chapter 5: Usenet News

Table 5-1 *Continued*: Commands for Using nn and trn

Action	NN	TRN	Notes
Enter a follow-up to a message	F	f or F	With trn, using F will include the text of the original message
Reply to a message via e-mail	R	r or R	With trn, using R will include the text of the original message
Mail the message to someone	M	M	
Save the message in a file	s	s	You then have to download the file to your PC

General:

Get help	H or :man	h	
Post a new message	:nnpost	!Pnews	
Go to specific newsgroup	G *newsgroup*	g *newsgroup*	
Subscribe/unsubscribe	U (while in group)	S or U (at Read Now? prompt)	

Reading Usenet News

- Decide whether to read new articles in the group.
- If yes, select articles from the list.
- When you finish going through the list, read the articles.
- Follow-up or reply to any articles.
- Go to the next newsgroup.

Sending Messages with nn and trn

When you edit a message to post to Usenet, nn will let you compose it in the Pico editor (this is why you have the EDITOR line in your .profile file). When you're finished writing, press Ctrl-X. Nn responds with the cryptic

Using the Internet

```
Save modified buffer (ANSWERING "No" WILL
DESTROY CHANGES) (y/n)?
```

Translation: Is the message OK? Chances are you'll answer Yes by pressing Y.

Nn then responds with something like

```
File Name to write : /tmp/snd.10006.
```

Don't worry about this; Pico is creating a temporary file before it sends your mail. Just press <Enter>.

If you're using trn, you'll use a special program called Pnews to compose a message, rather than the Pico editor.

Using Graphical Newsreaders

Graphical newsreaders (see Figure 5-2) allow you to do all the same things that the text-based nn and trn do, except you're within the Windows or Macintosh environment.

Using a graphical newsreader is similar to using a text-based one: You get a list of available newsgroups, choose the ones you want to subscribe to, and then read new messages each time you log on. Most graphical newsreaders will present you with a list of the newsgroups to which you have subscribed and indicate which of those have new messages. When you double-click on that newsgroup, it will list the new messages in date, subject, or thread order. Some will show both old and new messages, with the unread ones in a different color. When you double-click on a message, you can read it, and then reply or follow up.

Surprisingly, many people who have SLIP connections still use text-based newsreaders because they find them easier to use!

If you find, that graphical newsreaders aren't as easy to use as you had hoped, you can use nn or trn instead. Just telnet to your provider (i.e., **telnet provider.com**), log in with your username at the prompt, and enter your password. You should then be able to run nn, trn, or both, either by entering the respective name at the Unix prompt, or by choosing it from a menu, depending on what your provider offers.

Binary Postings

There are several Usenet newsgroups for posting binary files—pictures, sounds, movies, and the like. Here are two examples:

Chapter 5: Usenet News

```
alt.binaries.pictures.movies
comp.binaries.ibm.pc
```

You will see postings in that group that look like this (if you use nn):

```
f John Smith   217   "Close Encounters" 5tones.wav (1/4)
g John Smith   226   "Close Encounters" 5tones.wav (2/4)
h John Smith   209   "Close Encounters" 5tones.wav (3/4)
i John Smith    88   "Close Encounters" 5tones.wav (4/4)
```

If you try to read any of these files, you'll see gibberish. These are binary files that have been converted to text form by a process called *uuencoding*. In the example above, the file 5TONES.WAV (a sound file) has been converted into four separate text files. To reconstruct the file, you need to combine the four files into one, then use a uudecoder program to convert the file from text to its original, binary form.

Luckily, many newsreaders—including both nn and trn—will do this for you automatically. First, you select the posts that make up the file you want as if you were going to read them. Then tell your newsreader to decode them.

With nn, you enter **:decode**, then enter a period (to tell nn to put the decoded file in your home directory), and then press + to tell nn to decode all the files you have selected. If you've selected some nonbinary files along with the uuencoded ones, nn will simply skip them.

With trn, you simply enter **:e** and trn will decode the selected files. You then must press J to unmark them; for some reason trn doesn't do that automatically.

Many *graphical newsreaders* do not support automatic decoding of binary files. If they do, you'll have to check your software documentation to see what the procedure is. If not, you will have to read each message (the gibberish), save it in a single text file, and use a separate uudecoder to turn that text file into a picture, sound, or other file. Many Internet software packages come with separate uudecoders.

Tip: You can get more information about decoding binary files by reading the **alt.binaries.pictures.d** newsgroup.

65

Using the Internet

Usenet Netiquette

Just as there are unwritten rules of behavior for e-mail, so too are there guidelines for Usenet News.

Read the FAQ file. Before you ask a question in a Usenet newsgroup, check for the group's FAQ (Frequently Asked Questions) file. This is a periodic posting that lists all the questions that have been repeatedly asked and answered in the group; it is also posted to the **news.answers** newsgroup. With a couple of million people reading Usenet News every day and new people always joining in, the regulars in most newsgroups get tired of answering the same questions all the time, so they create a FAQ. And they get quite cross with people who storm in and ask one of those questions.

Quote back messages. Just as in e-mail—perhaps even more importantly—in Usenet you should quote back the messages to which you are replying. Many people will not have been following the conversation, and even those who have may not understand what you're replying to. Most newsreaders will automatically insert the original text, usually preceding it with an angle bracket and often with a phrase indicating where it came from:

```
John Smith <jsmith@bigcorp.com> had this to say:
> I think Internet World is the best magazine
> around, especially if the Net is a big part of
> your life.
```

You can then add your comment underneath, making it easier for people to follow the conversation:

```
John Smith <jsmith@bigcorp.com> had this to say:
> I think Internet World is the best magazine
> around, especially if the Net is a big part of
> your life.
You're not kidding! It's a great magazine—I read
it every month.
```

Quotes can sometimes get several messages deep:

```
Jane Doe <jane@another.corp.com.com> had this to say:
>John Smith <jsmith@bigcorp.com> had this to say:
```

Chapter 5: Usenet News

```
>> I think Internet World is the best magazine
>> around, especially if the Net is a big part of
>> your life.
>You're not kidding! It's a great magazine—I read it
>every month.
Where can I get this magazine? Does someone have a
phone number for subscriptions?
```

Don't advertise. Don't spam. You may have the greatest product in the history of the world and think that Usenet News is the best place to advertise it. You're wrong. Few will mind if you mention your ski equipment catalog in the **rec.skiing** group, but you'll anger a lot of people if you don't confine your message to only one or two appropriate groups. No one reading **alt.fan.dave-barry** wants to read about ski equipment, green cards, thigh cream, or how to make money fast.

If you do decide to tell people about your company, catalog, or whatever, don't make it a blatant ad; people get enough of that on television. The best thing to do is post a short "E-mail me for info" message, or tell them where and how to get more information. Don't force them to read it in a Usenet post.

Spamming is the Usenet term for posting the same message to more than a few newsgroups. The content isn't important; it doesn't matter if you're posting an ad for a ski chalet or a plea for peace on earth. No one wants to read the same thing over and over.

Usenet Resources

Be sure to subscribe to **news.announce.newusers**, **news.announce.important**, and **news.newusers.questions**. They're all good places for Internet newcomers.

Outside of Usenet, but still important, are the archives of Usenet FAQ files. The largest and best known are kept at the Massachusetts Institute of Technology. In order to access these files, you must use FTP (see Chapter 7). Use FTP to go to **rtfm.mit.edu** and look in the **/pub/usenet-by-group** directory. There you'll find the collected, up-to-date FAQ files from hundreds of Usenet newsgroups. You'll also find many FAQ files in the **/pub/usenet-by-group/news.answers** directory.

Using the Internet

Some Usenet Newsgroups to Try

Wondering what Usenet newsgroups to subscribe to? Table 5-2 lists the 25 most popular in terms of the number of subscribers:

Table 5-2: Usenet Newsgroup

Newsgroup	Description
news.announce.newusers	The place to go for the latest information, especially for newcomers; estimated over one million readers
rec.humor.funny	The moderated place for jokes and funny commentary
news.answers	The Usenet's repository for FAQ files
alt.sex	The name says it all
news.announce.important	The latest important news for everyone on the Net
alt.sex.stories	Tales rated R, X, or worse; not for the modest
misc.jobs.offered	Job listings from around the world
comp.lang.c	Discussions of programming
news.newusers.questions	Internet questions answered
comp.unix.questions	Unix questions answered
rec.humor	The unmoderated place for the latest jokes of all flavors
alt.binaries.pictures.erotica	Pictures of naked people (uuencoded)
news.groups	Information about new Usenet newsgroups
comp.risks	Discussion of Unix security problems and solutions
comp.lang.c++	Discussions of programming in the C++ language

Table 5-2 *Continued*: Usenet Newsgroups

Newsgroup	Description
news.announce.newgroups	Announcements of new Usenet newsgroups
alt.tv.simpsons	Talk about the popular Fox animated TV series
rec.arts.movies.reviews	Reviews of new and old motion pictures
alt.sex.bondage	Tie me up, tie me down...
misc.jobs.misc	People looking for and offering jobs
alt.bbs	Discussions of local bulletin board systems
rec.arts.startrek.info	Talk and information about ... well, you know
comp.os.linux.announce	Announcements about products for the Linux operating system
rec.arts.movies	General discussions about the latest flicks
rec.video	Talk about what's on videotape

Tip: The list of most popular newsgroups is posted periodically to *news.lists*.

CHAPTER SIX

internet
relay chat (IRC)

i f you want to talk with someone else on the Internet, you don't have to wait for your electronic mail to get through, or for them to get around to reading Usenet News. You can talk to people in real time, through your keyboard, using *Internet Relay Chat* or *IRC*.

IRC works a lot like a CB radio. You "tune in" a *channel* and join a few or even dozens of other people. Once tuned in, whatever you enter at your keyboard is displayed on the screens of all the other people on the channel, and vice versa. It's an ongoing, real-time conversation that can get pretty boisterous. IRC is not for the faint of heart.

Using the Internet

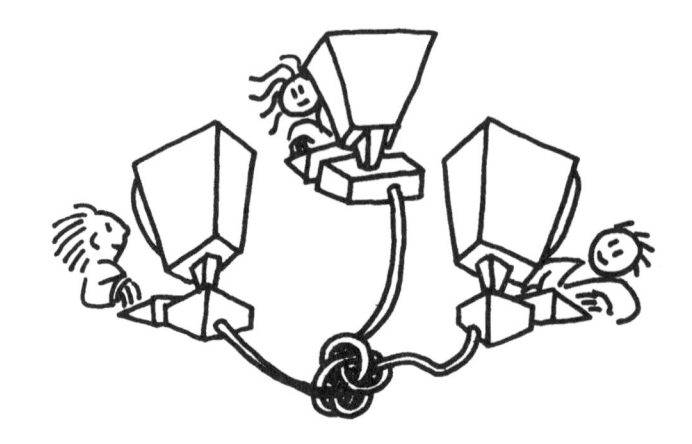

With IRC, you log into a special computer called a *chat server*. Once there, you choose a nickname for yourself and then select from one of thousands of channels (you can, of course, get a list). Some of those channels have discussions of current events, philosophy, recreation, sex, business, or anything else you can think of. There are also word and trivia games being played on IRC controlled by *bots*, short for "robots." (A bot is a software program that acts as a human moderator, prompting players when it's their turn to play or announcing when someone has won the game. Bots on nongame channels may scold you for using bad language or may automatically change the topic of the channel when they see certain words.)

IRC is a great way to get away from whatever you're doing for a few minutes—or a few hours. Although you can use it for business, perhaps having a virtual meeting with your colleagues around the world, most people use IRC for fun, not profit.

Using IRC

To use IRC, you need two things: an *IRC client* (the software that lets you talk) and access to an *IRC server*. If you have a shell account on a Unix system, you will probably use the simple but effective Unix IRC client that your provider should supply. To see if it does, enter **irc** at your Unix

Chapter 6: Internet Relay Chat

prompt. If that doesn't work, try **ircII** (capitalization counts!). If both these commands fail, try telnetting to **sci.dixie.edu 6677**, which is a public IRC site that you may be able to use—but no promises.

What's a Client?

You'll hear the term *client* a lot in this book and on the Net. A client is a piece of software that lets you get hold of a specific kind of information. IRC clients let you access Internet Relay Chat, Archie clients (see Chapter 7) let you use Archie to get information, and Gopher clients (see Chapter 8) let you get information from Gopher. You can usually substitute the word *software* when you see *client*.

If you have a SLIP/PPP or direct Internet connection, there are two ways you can use IRC. You can get hold of a Windows or Macintosh client for IRC and then find a server to connect to. Or you can use a shell account instead of your SLIP connection and use IRC from there. When you get a SLIP connection, most providers also give you a shell account. To access it, you telnet to your provider (**telnet provider.com**). At the login prompt, enter your username and then the password your provider supplied—the same one you use for your SLIP account. If this doesn't work, contact your provider to learn the procedure to use.

Why would you want to use a shell account to get to IRC? After all, you're paying for a SLIP connection, so why should you use a shell? Three reasons. First, IRC is all text anyway, so the advantages of a graphical IRC client are limited. Second, if you use a text-based Unix client, it will automatically connect you to a public IRC server that your provider knows about. With a graphical client, you have to seek out a server that will allow you to log on. Lastly, many commercial Internet packages do not include an IRC client but *do* include a telnet application, so you have to use FTP (see Chapter 7) to get a freeware or shareware package from the Net that you then have to install and configure.

Using the Internet

General IRC Commands

When you start a text-based IRC client (remember—the client is the software you run to use a service on the Internet, in this case IRC), you will see a message that reads something like this:

```
*** Connecting to port 6667 of server irc.provider.com
```

Some systems will immediately ask you to choose a name for yourself:

```
*** Please enter your nickname
Nickname:
```

You then specify your nickname or *handle*. It can be your name (Andrew) or anything else you want to be known as (Flyboy). If someone else on IRC is already using it, however, you'll be notified:

```
*** You have specified an illegal nickname
```

Other systems will show you a welcome screen immediately:

```
*** Welcome to the Internet Relay Network, AndrewK
*** If you have not already done so, please use /HELP NEWUSER
*** to read the new user information.
*** Your host is irc.provider.com, running version
    2.8.21+digi.pl6i
*** This server was created Sat Aug 8 1995 at 17:34:51 EDT
*** There are 4680 users and 3847 invisible on 111 servers
*** There are 116 operators online
*** 2254 channels have been formed
*** This server has 264 clients and 1 servers connected
```

If you haven't selected a nickname already, that's the first thing you do. At the bottom of the screen is the command line where you type instructions, in this case **/nick nickname**, where *nickname* is what you want to be called, as in **/nick AndrewK**. (All IRC commands start with a slash.) If you aren't told that your nickname is illegal, you're ready to go.

From this point you can get a list of available channels by typing **/list**, but because it's an awfully long list, try

Chapter 6: Internet Relay Chat

/list -MIN 10 -MAX 30 to get a list of channels with between 10 and 30 other users. (If you prefer a small conversation, you can use **/list -MAX 5**.)

When you know the name of a channel you want to join—either from the list or because you read about it—you can use the **/join** command. For instance, to join the popular #hottub channel, you would enter **/join #hottub**. (All channels are preceded by a pound sign.) A good channel to head for if you're feeling uncomfortable is **#irchelp**, where people are more willing to answer your questions.

When you join a channel, you'll see a message like this:

```
*** andrew (ak@panix.com) has joined channel #chatter
*** Topic for #chatter: Lots of talk about nothing!
*** Users on #chatter: andrew Betsy dagwood KAR120C Lollipop
newbie @chat_bot
```

> **Note:** Once you join a channel, everything you type that isn't preceded by a slash will be seen by everyone else on the channel—so be careful! You might want to start with a simple "Hello, all!" You can send private messages to other users by using the **/msg** command. So **/msg Kara Hi there!** would send the message "Hi there!" to Kara... no matter what channel she's on.

Use the command **/help** to get a list of help topics and learn about the other useful IRC commands, such as the ever popular **/quit**. See Table 6-1 for a summary of IRC commands.

Until you get used to it, IRC may look like just a jumble of messages. Besides notes from other people, there are messages from the server (informing you of people joining, people leaving, etc.) and assorted other things cluttering the screen. A plus sign in front of a person's nickname indicates that they are an operator (or op) on that channel, which means they can kick you off if they don't like your behavior. An asterisk in front of a message indicates that it comes from the server, not a person. See Figure 6-1.

Using the Internet

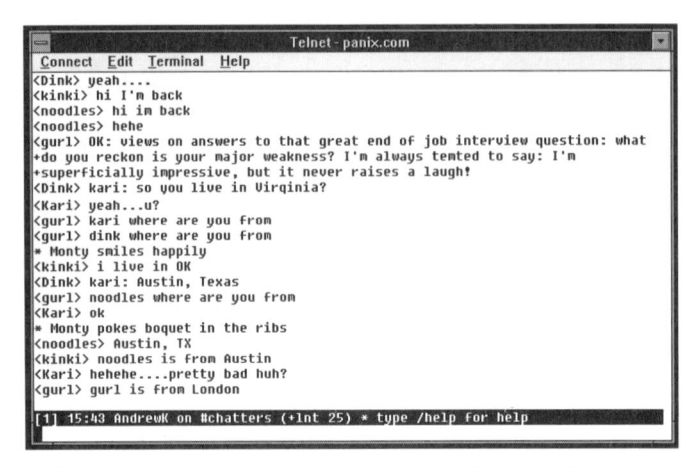

```
                    Telnet - panix.com
Connect  Edit  Terminal  Help
<Dink> yeah....
<kinki> hi I'm back
<noodles> hi im back
<noodles> hehe
<gurl> OK: views on answers to that great end of job interview question: what
+do you reckon is your major weakness? I'm always temted to say: I'm
+superficially impressive, but it never raises a laugh!
<Dink> kari: so you live in Virginia?
<Kari> yeah...u?
<gurl> kari where are you from
<gurl> dink where are you from
* Monty smiles happily
<kinki> i live in OK
<Dink> kari: Austin, Texas
<gurl> noodles where are you from
<Kari> ok
* Monty pokes boquet in the ribs
<noodles> Austin, TX
<kinki> noodles is from Austin
<Kari> hehehe....pretty bad huh?
<gurl> gurl is from London

[1] 15:43 AndrewK on #chatters (+lnt 25) * type /help for help
```

Figure 6-1 IRC is easy to use, even with a shell account. Here's what it looks like.

Table 6-1: IRC Commands Summary

COMMAND	FUNCTION
/nick	Change your nickname—the name displayed every time you write something.
/list	Show a (long!) list of available channels. Using modifiers can help. For instance, the command **/list -min 10 -max 25** will list all channels with between 10 and 25 people. And **/list -topic cats** will list all channels where the topic is cats.
/join *#channel*	Join the specified channel. All channels are preceded by a #.
/msg *nickname*	Send a private message to someone. For instance, **/msg ak Hey there**! would send the user with the nickname ak the message "Hey there!"—regardless of what channel the two of you are on.
/quit	Quits IRC.

Chapter 6: Internet Relay Chat

Graphical IRC

A graphical IRC client (Figure 6-2) works much the same way as the text-based version. Instead of typing in /**join #hottub**, however, you will select a command such as **Join** from a menu and then enter the channel. Other graphical clients may still require you to enter the commands, but will allow you to listen and talk to more than one channel at a time. Essentially, graphical clients use the same commands as text-based ones, but are prettier to look at and may have some additional features.

Where can you get a graphical IRC client, if it wasn't included in your software package? When you learn how to use FTP, you can download one from the Net. One of the best sites for this is at **cs-ftp.bu.edu** in the **/irc/clients/pc/windows** or **/macintosh** directories. Chapter 7 will explain how to use this information with FTP.

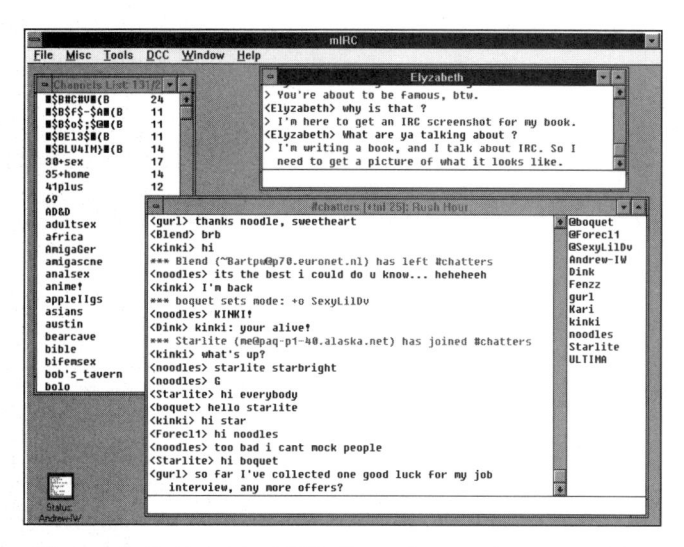

Figure 6-2 Graphical IRC clients let you keep up with several conversations at once but can get complicated.

Using the Internet

Once you have a graphical IRC client, you will need to find a server to connect to. Many clients have lists of servers built in, but that isn't true for all of them. The **cs-ftp.bu.edu** site also has a list of IRC servers; look in the **/irc/servers** directory.

CHAPTER SEVEN

anonymous ftp
and archie

Computers have files. The computer on your desk is full of them—everything from a poem you wrote, to your annual budget, to a game or two. In the same way, the millions of computers on the Internet also have files of every sort you can imagine. And the Internet lets you retrieve those files from the hard drives of all those computers (wherever they are, from across town to around the world) and move them to your own. The Internet works exactly the same way as a computer network in a small office but on a much larger scale.

With 5 million computers on the Net, it's not always easy to find the file you want. In the old days, when the Internet was new, everyone on it knew most of the other participants. If someone wanted a file, they simply called a colleague on

Using the Internet

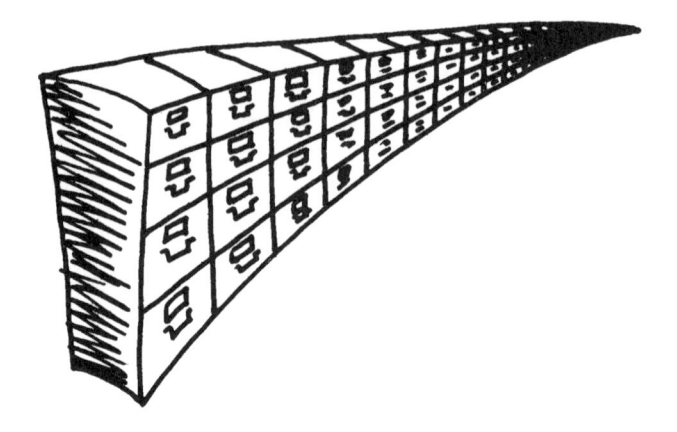

the phone and asked where it was. Today this process is much more difficult. There are too many people, too many computers, and too many files to be able to "keep it simple."

But it's not impossible. Magazines such as *Internet World* regularly publish FTP sites that have interesting files. You might see a listing like this: "A lot a good recipes are available via FTP at **ftp.bigcorp.com** in the **/pub/staff/jsmith** directory. The file is **food.txt**." That tells you the name of the computer, the directory (or folder, for you Mac folks) that contains the file, and the name of the file. If you communicate with people through e-mail or Usenet News, you will also hear from them about files that you want to get for yourself. To get these files, you use FTP.

Using FTP

FTP stands for *file transfer protocol*, which is a fancy name for the procedure you will use to hook up to another computer on the Internet and download the files that you want. It's often called *Anonymous FTP* because the computer you get the files from doesn't care who you are—you're anonymous.

Chapter 7: Anonymous FTP and Archie

To use FTP, you need to know three things: the name of the computer that has the file, the directory it's in, and the name of the file. In the section on Archie, we'll go over a way to find this information if you don't have it already.

The computer's name is a lot like an Internet e-mail address. It is separated into two or more parts by periods or dots. Examples of computer names are **bigcorp.com** and **ftp.whizkid.com**. The directory that contains the file is a series of words separated by slashes. An example of a directory is **/pub/windows/database**. Remember that Unix is case sensitive, especially when it comes to directory names.

If you have a shell account, you start an FTP session by entering **ftp** *sitename* at the Unix prompt—**ftp ftp.microsoft.com**, for instance.

If you have a SLIP/PPP connection, you start FTP by clicking on the appropriate icon. WinSock FTP is popular on Windows machines, and Fetch is the major FTP tool for the Macintosh.

No matter how you start FTP, it first connects you to the computer you specify. You might see a welcome message or a message to try again later. Once you connect, you will be asked to enter your username. Because this is anonymous FTP, you enter the username **anonymous**, and when asked for a password you enter your e-mail address.

Using the Internet

Once you have logged in, you must change to the directory that has the file you want by using the **cd** command, as in **cd /pub/windows/database**. You can then use Unix's **ls** command to get a list of available files.

If you're using a graphical FTP client over a SLIP connection, it will probably do the login procedure for you automatically. And rather than make you use the **ls** command, graphical FTP software usually automatically lists the available files and directories; to change directories you simply double-click on the directory you want to access. See Figure 7-1.

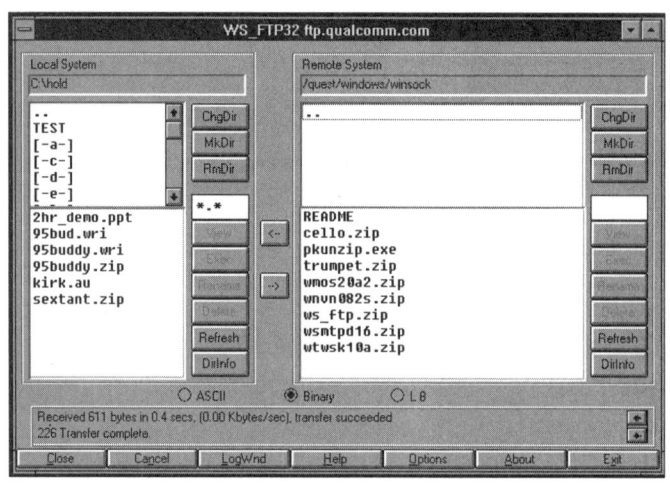

Figure 7-1 On the left is your hard drive; on the right is the other computer's. Transferring files is easy!

Once you find the right directory and see the file you want in the list of files, you get it—literally. The FTP command to retrieve a file is **get**, as in **get thatfile.txt**.

With a SLIP connection and a graphical client, you can highlight the file you want and then click on an arrow to retrieve it or, depending on the software, drag it from the list of files onto your hard drive.

If you are using a dial-up provider, you must then take the extra step of downloading the file from your provider's computer to the one on your desktop, using Unix's **sz** command. How long that takes depends on the speed of your modem.

Chapter 7: Anonymous FTP and Archie

> **FTP, 1-2-3**
>
> 1. Know the computer, directory, and file you want.
> 2. FTP to that site, as in **ftp ftp.bigcorp.com**.
> 3. Log in using the name **anonymous** and your e-mail address as the password (as in **jsmith@provider.com**), unless your software does that automatically.
> 4. Change to the right directory. With a shell account, enter **cd /directory/subdir** at the ftp> prompt. With SLIP access, simply double-click on the directory.
> 5. If the file you want is anything other than plain text (that is, having something other than a .txt extension), enter **binary** if you have a shell account.
> 6. Get the file you want. With a shell account, enter **get *filename***. Graphical clients use various methods of clicking on or dragging files.
> 7. If you have a shell account, download the file using the **sz** command or via a menu choice.

FTP by E-mail

Even if you don't have access to FTP for some reason, you can still retrieve files by using electronic mail. This process is best used for retrieving text files only; although you can—with a good deal of work—retrieve binary files, as well, such as games and pictures. The process is complicated and beyond the scope of this book.

FTP by e-mail is fairly straightforward. You need to know the computer that has the file you want, the directory it's in, and the name of the file.

To retrieve it, send a four-line e-mail message to either **ftpmail @decwrl.dec.com** or to **bitftp.pucc.princeton.edu**. In your message,

- The first line should read **connect *site***, where *site* is the name of the computer (such as ftp.bigcorp.com) that has the file you want.

Using the Internet

- The second line should read **chdir** */directory/ subdir*, where */directory/subdir* is the specific directory with the file you want.
- The third line should read **get** *filename*, where *filename* is the exact name of the file you want. (Remember: Unix is case sensitive.)
- The last line should be **quit**.

Your file will arrive in your mailbox in anywhere from a few hours to a few days, depending on how many people are using the FTP-by-mail server.

Dot *What*?

Often, when you search through another computer looking for files, you'll come upon some with unfamiliar file name extensions. There are a lot. Standards have emerged, however, and most of the files you encounter will have one of the extensions in Table 7-1.

Table 7-1: Common File Extensions

Extension	Definition
.txt	Likely a plain ASCII text file, easily readable by PCs and Macintoshes.
.gif, .jpg	GIF and JPEG files are the most popular types of pictures. They can be photographs, drawings, or other still images.
.mpg, .avi, .mov	Three standards for motion video. MPEG is the most common.
.hqx, .sea	Macintosh compressed files. You'll need a version of StuffIt to uncompress .hqx files; .sea files are self-extracting archives.
.zip	PC compressed files. You'll need PKUnzip to uncompress them.
.Z	Standard Unix compressed file. Unix's **uncompress** command should work.
.gz	File compressed with the GZip program. The Unix program **gunzip** will uncompress it.

Chapter 7: Anonymous FTP and Archie

Good FTP Sites

There are thousands of FTP sites around the world. Some have a few files for downloading by the public, and some are major archives—computers whose administrators have filled their hard disks with useful software and other information. Here are some popular sites.

WUArchive

The WUArchive at Washington University in St. Louis (**wuarchive.wustl.edu**) is probably the largest repository of software for PCs and Macs in the world. Unfortunately, it's not always easy to get in. When you do, however, check out the **/systems** subdirectories for your type of computer.

CICA

The **/pub/pc/win3** directory at **ftp.cica.indiana.edu** is one of the best places to find Windows software, especially freeware and shareware for use with a SLIP/PPP connection (in the **/pub/pc/win3/winsock** directory). You'll find e-mail software, newsreaders, and FTP and Gopher clients, plus some more esoteric programs. Because the site is so popular, it is *mirrored* at other sites (meaning that the files on CICA are also carried on other computers). When you log in, you might see a message informing you that CICA isn't accepting any more anonymous users for the time being. It will provide you with a list of mirror sites to try.

> **Note:** Freeware is software that can be used and distributed without charge. Shareware software must be registered and paid for in order to continue to use it. The fee is nominal and usually gives the user access to technical support, updates, and documentation.

Sumex-Aim

The Macintosh counterpart to CICA, Sumex-Aim (**sumex-aim.stanford.edu**) has piles upon piles of Mac freeware and shareware, from antivirus software to games, sound utilities, and more—all in the **/info-mac** directory.

Using the Internet

The Internet Society

The Internet Society maintains some useful information about the Internet at **ftp.isoc.org** in the **/isoc/charts** directory. You'll find statistics, charts, and the like.

RTFM

If it's information you want, check out the RTFM site at the Massachusetts Institute of Technology (**rtfm.mit.edu**). In the **/pub/usenet** directory you'll find information and frequently asked questions (and answers) from hundreds of Usenet newsgroups. If you have a question about anything, you're likely to find an answer there.

All About Archie

If you know there is a file out there somewhere on the Internet, but you don't know the exact location or name, you can use a program called Archie to search for it. There are machines called *Archie servers* that actually keep a record of all the files available all over the Internet. Using Archie means asking one of these servers to find files for you, by telling it what words to look for in the filename. If you want a copy of the game Wolfenstein, for example, you can ask Archie to search for the word *wolf*.

Most Internet access providers offer Archie on their systems, so all you need to do is enter the word **archie** at the

Chapter 7: Anonymous FTP and Archie

prompt and then part of the filename you are searching for (as in **archie wolf**). You can use the Unix command **man archie** (see Chapter 3) to learn other ways of using Archie. (The command **archie -s** *word* is the most useful; it tells Archie to ignore capitalization in the words you're looking for.)

There are also graphical Archie clients that let you enter the search term in a box and automatically retrieve a file for you. See Figure 7-2.

If your provider does not offer Archie, you can use telnet to go to a computer that does. By telnetting to **archie.internic.net** or **archie.unl.edu** and logging in as archie, you can enter an Archie query. At the archie> prompt, simply enter **find** *word* (i.e., **find wolf**) to search.

After you ask Archie to find a file for you, it responds with a list of computers that have files matching your request. It tells you the computer's name, the directory the file is in, and the exact filename. You can then use Anonymous FTP to retrieve the file.

The results of an Archie search for wolf might look like this:

```
Host freebsd.cdrom.com
  Location: /.13/mac/wuarchive/da
  FILE -r--r--r-- 25088 Mar 2 1988
    wolfpack.sit
  Location: /.3/games/msdos/arcade
  FILE -rw--rw--r-- 745670 Feb 4 1993
    1wolf14.zip Location: /.5/cica/sounds
  FILE -r--r--r-- 99121 Oct 27 1993
    wolfwavs.zip

Host ftp.njit.edu
  Location: /pub/images
  FILE -rw-r—r— 457150 Mar 27 1992
    wolfchess.gif
  FILE -rw-r--r-- 80949 Mar 19 1992
    wolfchess.ras.Z

Host ftp.wustl.edu
  Location: /multimedia/images/gif/t
```

Using the Internet

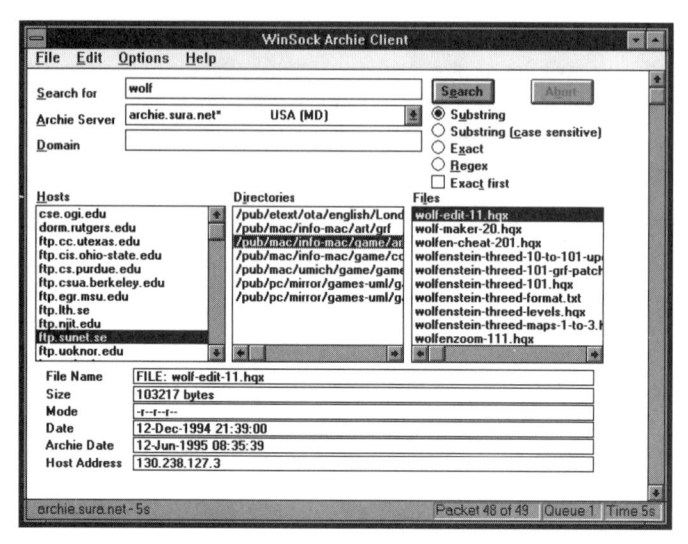

Figure 7-2 Archie will search the Net for a file you want.

```
FILE -rw-r--r-- 27751 Feb 10 1993
   timberwolf.gif
FILE -rw-r--r-- 27944 Feb 10 1993
   timberwolf2.gif
Location: /usenet/comp.binaries.ibm.pc/
   volume18
DIRECTORY drwxr-xr-x 8192 Oct 31 1993
   1wolf3d
```

In the foregoing listing, the Host is the name of the computer that has the files; that's the site to which you FTP. The Location is the directory that houses the file. And the line that begins with FILE tells you that Archie has found a file (or sometimes a DIRECTORY), some information about how the administrator has set it up (you don't need to worry about it), the size of the file, the date of the file, and its name.

Let's say you wanted to get the timberwolf.gif file from this entry:

```
   Host ftp.wustl.edu
   Location: /multimedia/images/gif/t
FILE -rw-r--r-- 27751 Feb 10 1993
   timberwolf.gif
```

You would first FTP to **ftp.wustl.edu**. Then change directory (using the **cd** command or by double-clicking on the appropriate directories, depending on whether you're using text-based or graphical FTP software) to the **/multimedia/images/gif/t** directory. Then use the **get** command to retrieve the file.

> **Whenfore Archie?**
>
> Archie is a great program to use when you want a particular *file* from the Internet. But Archie won't necessarily help you find the *information* you want, unless you know the name of the file it's in. So if you're looking for a copy of the game Doom, Archie is great. But if you just want the population of Fiji, you'll find it easier to use Gopher or the World Wide Web (see Chapters 8 and 9, respectively).

Surfer's Diary: Interesting and Useful FTP Sites

Address	Directory	Description
ftp.microsoft.com	/pub	Microsoft add-ons and updates
ftp.thelist.com	[none]	List of Internet providers

Surfer's Diary: Interesting and Useful FTP Sites

Address	Directory	Description

CHAPTER EIGHT

gopher and Veronica

*i*f you want information from the Internet—anything from the population of Fiji to the best restaurants in Sydney, Australia—it doesn't matter what name the file has. You want the *information*, not the file. And most of the time you won't even *know* the name of the file. What *would* be the filename for the population of Fiji, anyway?

In the beginning, the Internet was just a lot of files. As it grew, and with it the demand for information, some ways of organizing the information in those files became necessary. Gopher was one of them.

Using the Internet

Gopher Is Your Guide

In 1991, computer users at the University of Minnesota designed a system that made it easier for people to find the files they wanted amidst the millions. They created an indexing system called Gopher. With Gopher, computer administrators designed menus for users to follow to get the file they wanted. For instance, if you wanted information about Toyota Corolla gas mileage, you could go to a Toyota Gopher site, choose Corolla from a menu, and then Gas Mileage from another menu to see the information you wanted. Gopher helps you find your way.

In the old days, if Toyota wanted to provide online information about its cars, it could simply create files called corolla.txt, tercel.txt, camry.txt, and the like, and try to convince people to download them. But with Gopher, Toyota could organize that information in menus so that anyone with the right software—a *Gopher client*—could read them. And because the University of Minnesota distributed Gopher clients far and wide, everyone had one.

A Gopher menu reads just like a numbered list. On a client, Toyota's fictional *Gopher server* might look like this:

```
Internet Gopher Information Client v1.3
Root gopher server: cars.toyota.com
```

Chapter 8: Gopher and Veronica

```
1. Camry Information/
2. Corolla Information/
3. Paseo Information/
4. Tacoma Information/
5. Tercel Information/
6. Other Truck Information/
7. Toyota Leasing Plans.
8. Who to Contact.
9. Other Car Company Gophers/
```

Some choices on a menu may lead to another organization's Gopher server, and that other server may be in another city or another country. (In fact, any menu choice that has a slash at the end leads to another menu.)

You will find that many different kinds of organizations make information available through Gopher because it is so easy to do. Colleges and universities put everything from class schedules to local restaurant menus on their Gopher servers. Governments publish policy statements and news releases on their Gophers, and corporations put up product and sales information.

Using Gopher

Because Gopher is such a simple system, there is little difference between text-based and graphical clients.

To use Gopher, all you do is enter **gopher** at the Unix prompt; if you want to go to a specific site, you enter **gopher** *site*, as in **gopher gopher.panix.com**. If you have a graphical interface, you can double-click on the Gopher icon or even use a graphical World Wide Web browser (Chapter 9) to view Gopher menus. See Figure 8-1.

Most of the time, the first Gopher menu you see will be at the University of Minnesota, especially if you're using a text-based client. (Graphical clients may start at a Gopher server run by the company that makes the graphical software.) From there, you can choose from the menu and make your way to Gopher servers around the country and around the world.

Using the Internet

If you don't have Gopher software on your system, don't worry. You can use telnet to log into a public Gopher server. Type (or select) **telnet gopher.msu.edu**, and you'll be brought to the Michigan State University's Gopher system. (For more information about telnet, see Chapter 3.)

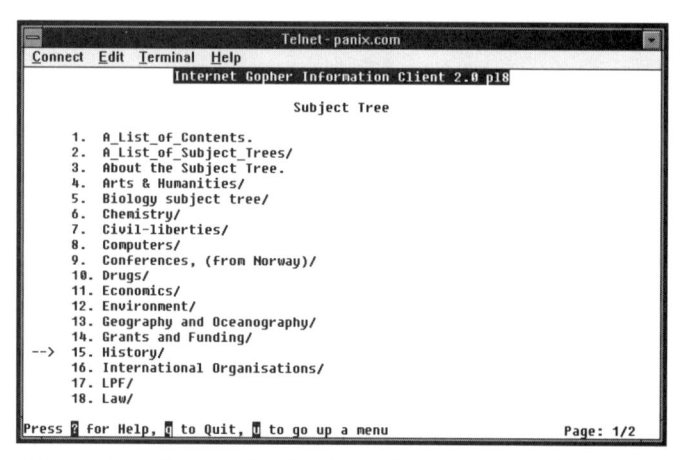

Figure 8-1 Gopher is simple and easy to use—just choose from a menu.

Table 8-1: Basic Gopher Commands

Command	Function
<up>, <down>	Navigate between menu items
<Enter> or type in item number	Select a menu item
u	Go back to the previous menu
m	E-mail the current item
s	Save the current item in a file
?	Get help
q	Quit

Chapter 8: Gopher and Veronica

Gopher Via a Web Browser

We'll cover World Wide Web browsers in the next chapter, but it's important to note here that many people with SLIP/PPP connections use a Web browser to view Gopher pages, rather than use two pieces of software.

To tell a Web browser to view a Gopher page, you precede the Gopher address with **gopher://**. For instance, to tell a browser to view the **gopher.panix.com** Gopher page, you would enter **gopher://gopher.panix.com** in the browser's address box.

Veronica

With all the information available on Gopher servers, it can be difficult to find the particular bit of data you are looking for. To that end, there is Veronica. Just as Archie searches for files available via FTP, Veronica searches Gopherspace for Gopher menu items that match a search term. Veronica searches are built into many Gopher servers; to find one, you need only browse around Gopher for a short time. You will eventually come across an item such as Veronica Search or Search Gopherspace Using Veronica. When you select that, you'll be prompted for a search term. Enter the term, and Veronica will search all of Gopherspace and provide you with a list of appropriate Gopher sites.

You might also find a Gopher item called Jughead (no joke!). Jughead works much like Veronica but searches only a single computer's Gopher-accessible files. Veronica searches all—or at least most—of the Gopher menus out there.

Good Gopher Sites

In recent years, Gopher has been overshadowed by the popular World Wide Web, and many Gopher sites have been converted to Web sites. There are, however, some good sources of information available through the Net's favorite rodent.

Gopher *subject trees* are lists of resources sorted by category. One of the better trees is available at **gopher.sunet.se**. It has entries for over a dozen categories and acts as a good starting point for exploring Gopherspace. You may want to

Using the Internet

use that subject tree—or the one at **inform.umd.edu**—as your Gopher startoff point.

With a shell account, enter **gopher gopher.sunet.se** at the prompt. Or create an alias in your .profile or .cshrc file—see Chapter 3—that reads **alias gopher gopher gopher.sunet.se**. With a graphical client, there will be a way to set your default Gopher site to one of the subject trees.

Gopher Jewels (gopher to **cwis.usc.edu**, select **Other Gophers and Information Resources**, then **Gopher Jewels**) is a continually updated list of interesting Gopher sites and resources. It's always worth checking out.

Gopher is a great tool for getting text-based information. But it is only a first step. The next step is the World Wide Web.

Surfer's Diary: Interesting and Useful Gopher Sites

Address	Directory	Description

Surfer's Diary: Interesting and Useful Gopher Sites

| Address | Directory | Description |

CHAPTER NINE

the world-wide
web

he World-Wide Web is also called simply the Web, or WWW or W3. Like Gopher, it began as an easier way for users of the Internet to find and view information. Whereas Gopher is divided into menus and submenus, every *page* (screen) of the Web acts as a menu. Those pages can contain text and pictures, and—most importantly—*links* to other pages on the Web. If you're reading a page of the Web, you can select a link (by either clicking on it or typing a command) and instantly be reading an entirely different page with its own text, pictures, and yet another set of links.

Imagine reading an article about Canada in *The New York Times*. Let's say there's a paragraph about the Vancouver Canucks hockey team. Touch the word *Canucks* with your

Using the Internet

mouse, and the newspaper page will instantly transform into a page of information about the team. And on that page you can touch the names of the players to get information about each one of them. That's how the Web works; each page has connections, called *hyperlinks*, to other pages.

On the Web, people and organizations—from elementary school students to major corporations—are creating Web pages and putting them on the Internet. Those pages contain anything you can imagine: personal information, corporate data, and pictures and graphics of every sort. The Web allows anyone to become a worldwide publisher, and it lets everyone create links from their pages to anyone else's. (You can link from your page to someone else's, but you can't change their page to link to yours.)

For instance, suppose some college students in California are big Robert Redford fans. They can write some information about him (a biography, filmography, etc.), collect some pictures, and create a Web page of their own so the whole world can see their work. On that page, there might be a reference to Redford's 1984 movie *The Natural*. Then, if the students find out that, say, the Iowa City Film Lovers' Club also has a Web page with information about *The Natural*, they can create a link from their Robert Redford page to the ICFLC's *The Natural* page.

The Natural was about baseball, so the ICFLC's page—besides providing information about the movie—might have a link to the National Baseball Hall of Fame's Web site in Cooperstown, NY. And that site may have links to home pages for all the major league baseball teams.

When you choose the link to a new page, either by selecting its number or clicking in the right place, you go there almost instantly. And that new page may also have links to still more pages.

Another reason for the popularity of the Web is that it is the only place on the Internet where advertising is accepted almost without reservation. Hundreds of companies, large and small, have created Web sites—not only to give corporate and product information to anyone who stops by, but also to sell their products through the Net! Instead of ordering flowers over the phone, you can do so over the Net (see Figure 9-1). Just click on your order,

Chapter 9: The World-Wide Web

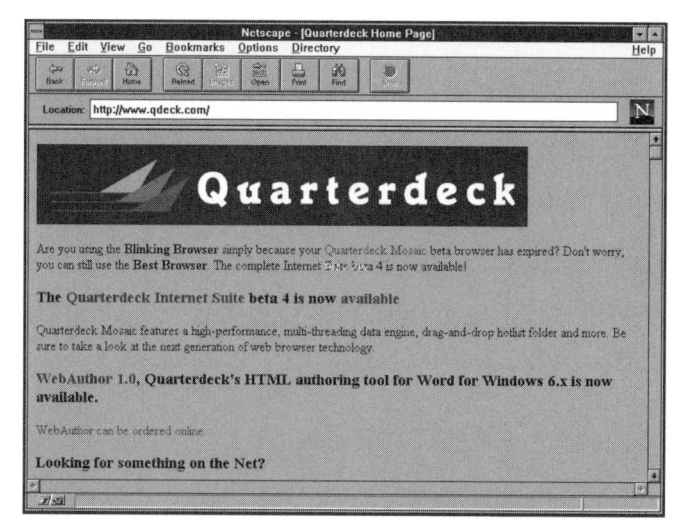

Figure 9-1 Companies like Quarterdeck find the Web an easy place to erect billboards — electronic ones.

enter your credit card number, and wait for delivery. Thanks to a variety of security measures, it's actually safer to give your credit card information to many Net-based stores than it is to give it over the phone.

How They Fit Together

People often get confused about the relationship between the Internet, the World-Wide Web, and products such as Mosaic and Netscape.

The World-Wide Web is *part* of the Internet; the Web is a group of files (called "pages") and the Internet is the way those files are transferred to your computer. Mosaic and Netscape are programs that let you view those Web pages over the Internet.

When someone says "I found this information on the World-Wide Web," what that means is "I used Mosaic or Netscape to transfer a page that's on the Web to my computer so I could view it."

Think of it in terms of getting a package in the mail. The package itself is the page of the Web. It is brought to you by a truck (Netscape or Mosaic) and that truck uses the highway system (the Internet) to get it to you. You need both a truck and a highway to get your package (you need both a Web browser and the Internet to view a Web page).

103

Using the Internet

Using the Web

If you want to use the World-Wide Web, you need a piece of software called a Web *browser*. Just as there are different programs for e-mail, Usenet News, and Gopher, there are different products to use the Web. Your Web browser might be a piece of software you get for your PC or Mac, or it might be something your Internet access provider offers.

There are two basic kinds of browsers: text and graphical. *If you have a shell account,* you will use a browser that your provider supplies. It will be text-based, so you won't be able to see any of the pictures on the Web or easily download any of the sound or video files there. But you don't need a special connection to use one of the text browsers, which is why many people on the Net still use one.

If you have a SLIP/PPP or direct connection to the Internet, you can use any one of over 20 graphical Web browsers, some of which—like Mosaic and Netscape—you may have heard of. They will allow you to see the pictures and graphics that have made the Web so popular.

Note: Shell accounts and SLIP/PPP connections are explained in Chapter 2.

No matter what kind of browser you have, using the Web is a pretty simple process. You view pages, and those pages have links; if you want to follow a link, you can select it either with your mouse or with a keyboard command. You can find out the address of the page you're viewing, also, and save that page so you can go back to it another time. You can also save the text of a page or e-mail it to someone.

All Web browsers use *uniform resource locators* or *URLs* to tell them what page on the Web to display. A URL can be a Web page, a Gopher menu, FTP site, or Usenet newsgroup (more on that in a moment). All addresses—or URLs—of pages on the World-Wide Web follow the same pattern: **http://*computer***. Sometimes it will be **http://*computer*/*directory*** or **http://*computer.name*/*directory*/*file***. Here are some examples:

104

Chapter 9: The World-Wide Web

    http://www.bigcorp.com
    http://www.bigcorp.com/public
    http://www.bigcorp.com/public/events.html

Using a Text Browser

If you have a Unix shell account, there are two programs you can use to access the Web: the Line-Mode Browser and Lynx. Neither will allow you to see pictures or some of the nice formatting of many Web pages, but you will be able to read the text and follow the links—the most important things.

The Line-Mode Browser

The original browser for the World-Wide Web is now known as the *Line-Mode Browser* (see Figure 9-2). I won't spend much time on it because (a) it's awful, and (b) it's becoming harder and harder to find because Lynx (see below) has replaced it as the text-based Unix Web browser of choice.

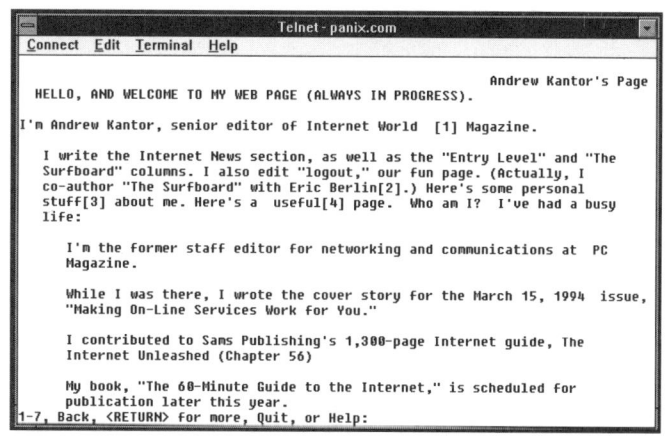

```
                                Telnet - panix.com
 Connect   Edit   Terminal   Help

                                                        Andrew Kantor's Page
   HELLO, AND WELCOME TO MY WEB PAGE (ALWAYS IN PROGRESS).

 I'm Andrew Kantor, senior editor of Internet World   [1] Magazine.

   I write the Internet News section, as well as the "Entry Level" and "The
   Surfboard" columns. I also edit "logout," our fun page. (Actually, I
   co-author "The Surfboard" with Eric Berlin[2].) Here's some personal
   stuff[3] about me. Here's a  useful[4] page. Who am I?  I've had a busy
   life:

        I'm the former staff editor for networking and communications at  PC
        Magazine.

        While I was there, I wrote the cover story for the March 15, 1994  issue,
        "Making On-Line Services Work for You."

        I contributed to Sams Publishing's 1,300-page Internet guide, The
        Internet Unleashed (Chapter 56)

        My book, "The 60-Minute Guide to the Internet," is scheduled for
        publication later this year.
 1-7, Back, <RETURN> for more, Quit, or Help:
```

Figure 9-2 You hardly see it anymore, but the Linemode browser is how most people used to view the World-Wide Web.

To use the Line-Mode Browser, you can probably enter **www** at your Unix prompt. If there is a specific page on the Web you want to reach—maybe you read about it in

Using the Internet

Internet World or heard about it on Usenet News—use the command **www** *page*, as in

```
www http://www.panix.com/~ak
```

On the page you'll see the page text with occasional numbers in square brackets; these indicate the links. To follow one, simply type its number at the command line on the bottom.

The Line-Mode Browser commands are listed in Table 9-1.

Table 9-1: Line-Mode Browser Commands

Command	Description
<*number*>	Follow the numbered link
b	Go back one page
go *address*	Go to the specified URL (as in **go http://www.bigcorp.com**)
l	List the pages to which this document is linked
> *filename*	Save the text of this document in a file
h	Get help
q	Quit

Lynx

Very few people use the Line-Mode Browser anymore because of the popularity and simplicity of Lynx (see Figure 9-3). Although it's also text-based, Lynx is easier to use and certainly easier to look at. And, just as with Gopher, if your provider doesn't offer Lynx, you can telnet to it and log on to another computer. Just telnet to **ukanaix.cc.ukans.edu** and log in as **www**. (For more about telnet, see Chapter 3.)

With Lynx you see the text of a Web page, but the links are in boldface. You can use your <Up> and <Down> arrow keys to highlight the next and previous links, respectively. Although Lynx may not be up to par with graphical Web browsers, it's not a bad place to start.

Basic Lynx commands are listed in Table 9-2.

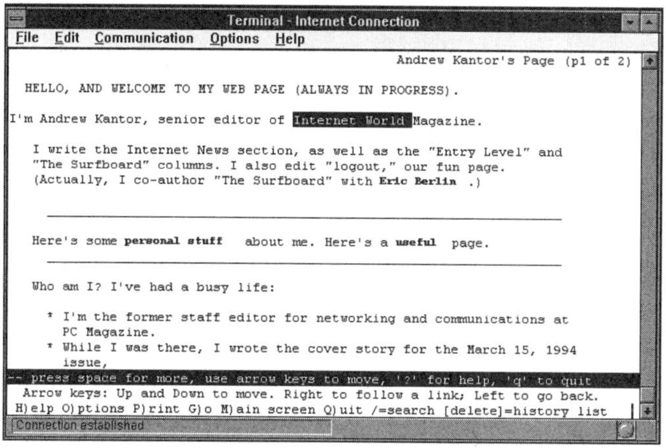
Terminal - Internet Connection
File Edit Communication Options Help
Andrew Kantor's Page (p1 of 2)
HELLO, AND WELCOME TO MY WEB PAGE (ALWAYS IN PROGRESS).
I'm Andrew Kantor, senior editor of Internet World Magazine.
I write the Internet News section, as well as the "Entry Level" and
"The Surfboard" columns. I also edit "logout," our fun page.
(Actually, I co-author "The Surfboard" with Eric Berlin .)
Here's some personal stuff about me. Here's a useful page.
Who am I? I've had a busy life:
* I'm the former staff editor for networking and communications at
PC Magazine.
* While I was there, I wrote the cover story for the March 15, 1994
issue,
-- press space for more, use arrow keys to move, '?' for help, 'q' to quit
Arrow keys: Up and Down to move. Right to follow a link; Left to go back.
H)elp O)ptions P)rint G)o M)ain screen Q)uit /=search [delete]=history list
Connection established

Figure 9-3 Lynx is the most popular of the remaining Unix-based Web browsers, supplanting the old Line-Mode Browser.

Table 9-2: Lynx Commands

COMMAND	DESCRIPTION
+ or <Spacebar>	Scroll down through document
-, b	Scroll up ("back") through document
<Down> / <Up>	Select next/previous link
<Enter> or <Right>	Follow a link
<Left>	Go back to previous page
p	Save or mail text of file
a	Add current page to your bookmark file
v	View your bookmarks
=	Find out the address of the page you're viewing
o	Set Lynx options
? or h	Get help
q / Q	Quit/Fast Quit

Using the Internet

Using a Graphical Browser

Graphical browsers show you pictures and make choosing links easy. In addition, they often have other features to make your travels on the Web both fun and productive. You can choose among over 20 graphical Web browsers—many for Windows, some for Macs, and a few for OS/2 and even Amiga computers. Although there are significant differences between MacWeb, WinWeb, Mosaic, Cello, and Netscape, for example, all graphical browsers let you do similar things.

Note: Remember that you need a SLIP or PPP connection to use a graphical Web browser.

When you start a graphical browser, it loads a default home page—the Web page that the browser company has selected for you to start with (see Figures 9-4 and 9-5). Often it is the home page for that particular company. You can always change the Web page at which you start. Some browsers require you to go to an Options or Configuration menu to do this, and some older ones require you to edit a file (such as MOSAIC.INI) on your hard drive.

Most browsers will display a page's text and graphics, but if you have a slow modem, you may want to choose the menu item that tells the browser not to display graphics. Because they are much larger than text, you can speed up the load time of graphics-heavy pages by telling your browser not to retrieve pictures.

When a page is displayed, the links will be blue or some other contrasting color. You'll see both highlighted text and, possibly, pictures with blue borders that also act as links. To select one, simply click on it with your mouse. As you move your cursor over a link, the cursor arrow will probably change—to a hand, most likely—indicating that you can click there. You might also see the address to which that link points, on the bottom of the screen.

As you follow links, you will often want to go back to a previous page. Most browsers have a Back button or menu choice to let you do just that. They also have Home buttons to take you to your startup page.

Chapter 9: The World-Wide Web

Figure 9-4 Here's how my old home page looked in Lynx ...

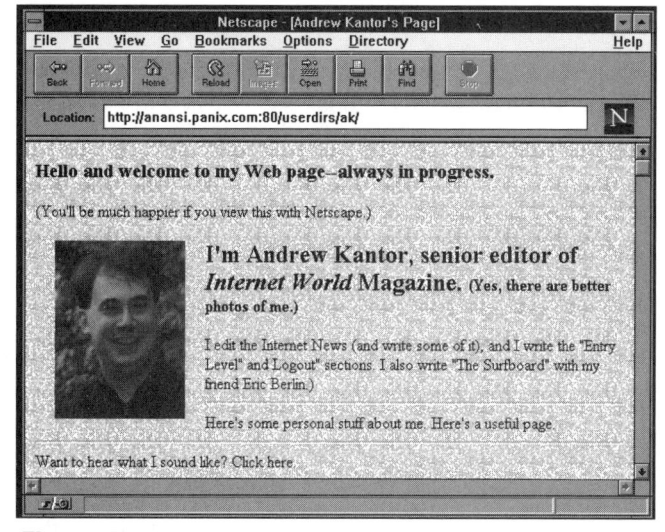

Figure 9-5 ... and here's the same page under Netscape.

Maybe you want to go to a Web page whose address you already know; the browser lets you go directly there. Some graphical browsers have a box on the screen for you to type in the URL of the page you want, and others require you to choose an item from the File menu such as Open Location or Go to URL (Figure 9-6). If you can't figure out how to go to a specific page, check your browser's Help file.

109

Using the Internet

If you find yourself on a page that you'd like to return to later, graphical browsers allow you to keep track of your favorite spots with a *hotlist* or *bookmarks*. When you're viewing a page you like, you'll be able to choose from a menu item such as Bookmarks, Hotlist, or Personal Favorites to add that page to your hotlist or to go to favorite pages you've already added.

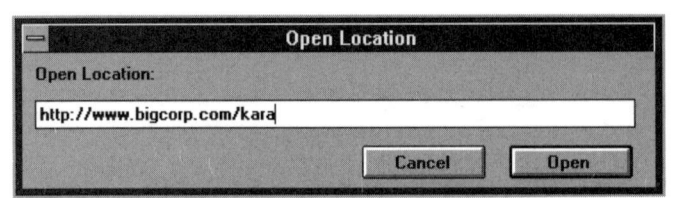

Figure 9-6 The address of a Web page is called a Uniform Resource Locator or URL. Enter it in your Web browser and off you go.

Finally, graphical browsers allow you to print the page you're looking at. (Yes, text-based browsers may let you do this as well, but without the pretty pictures.) Just choose Print from the File menu.

All-in-One

Besides being able to display Web pages, many graphical Web browsers can view Gopher pages and even allow you to retrieve files via FTP. (See Figures 9-7 and 9-8.) Some even allow you to read Usenet News.

Just as pages on the Web all begin with **http://**, you can specifiy a Gopher menu by using **gopher://**, as in

```
gopher://gopher.panix.com
```

Your browser will display a Gopher menu much as any graphical Gopher client would; you can click on a menu item to have it displayed.

You can also use many browsers for FTP by entering **ftp://***computer*/*directory*, as in

```
ftp://rtfm.mit.edu/pub/usenet
```

Chapter 9: The World-Wide Web

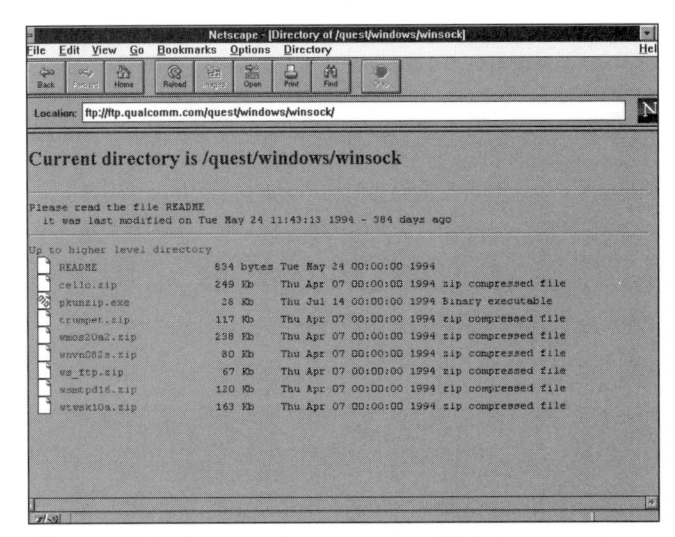

Figure 9-7 You can also use many Web browsers to do file transfers with Anonymous FTP.

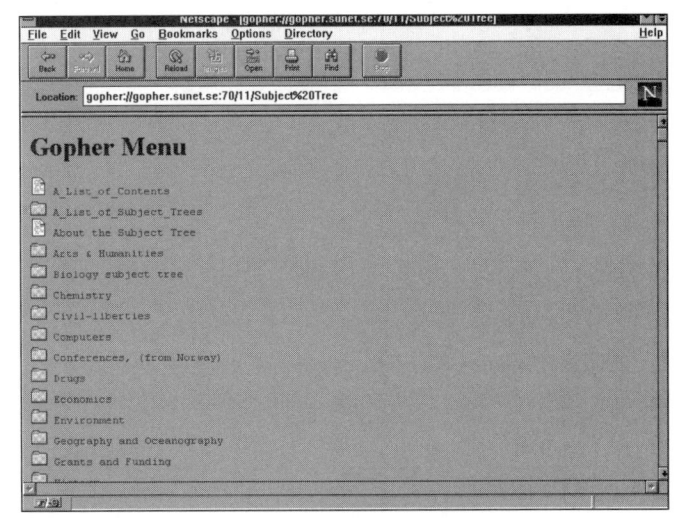

Figure 9-8 Gopher is aging, but most graphical Web browsers will let you view Gopher menus.

Using the Internet

You'll see a list of available subdirectories and files. Click on a subdirectory to go there; click on a file to download it to your computer.

Some graphical browsers, such as Netscape, also allow you to read Usenet News. By using **news://***newsgroup* as the URL, you can read and reply to Usenet messages. You will have to configure Netscape properly; using the Options menu, and tell it the address of your News server. As described in Chapter 5, this is information your Internet provider can supply.

Getting Two Web Browsers—Free!

You can download from the Internet the two most well-known World-Wide Web browsers. Mosaic is available at **ftp.ncsa.uiuc.edu** in the **/Mosaic/Windows** or **/Mosaic/Mac** directories. Download and read a README file in the directory to find out what files to download and how to install the software.

Netscape is available at **ftp.netscape.com** in the **/netscape/windows** or **/netscape/mac** directories. Again, make sure to look at the README file first.

Good Web Sites

There are thousands of pages on the Web. Some are fun, some are useful, and some just take up space. Here are nine of the more useful ones.

Note: These addresses are current as of the time we went to press. But the Net is always changing, so there's no guarantee these pages will still be there when you check them out.

Chapter 9: The World-Wide Web

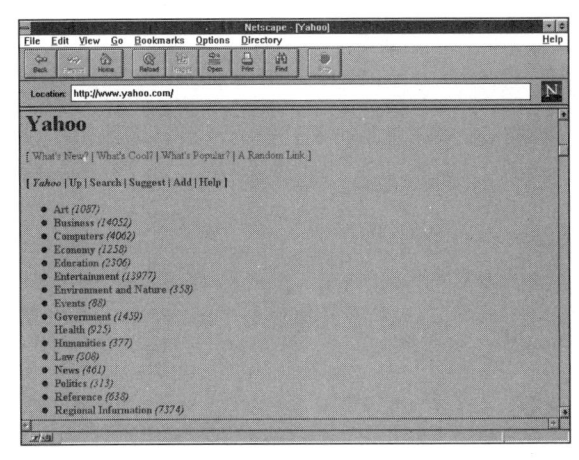

Yahoo (http://www.yahoo.com)

Yahoo is one of, if not *the* best, resource on the World-Wide Web. Essentially, it's a catalog of much of the Web, sorted by category. There is also a search tool that lets you enter a keyword and provides links to other Web search engines in case you can't find what you want. Yahoo is a great candidate for your default home page.

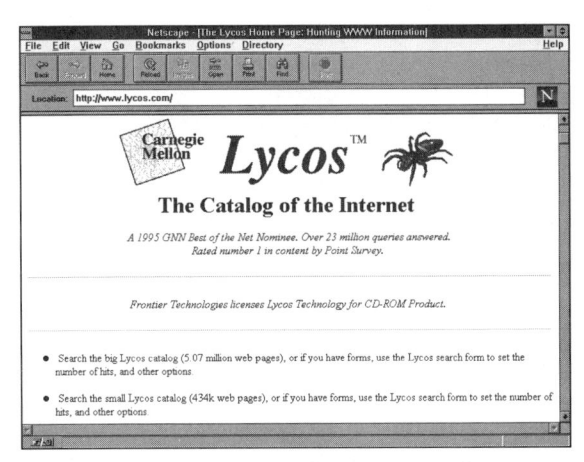

Lycos (http://www.lycos.com)

Next to Yahoo, the most comprehensive search tool for the Web is Lycos, hosted by Carnegie-Mellon University. Although it's often busy, Lycos is a great way to find the information you want. It contains two separate search sets: small and large. Using either, you're bound to find what you're looking for.

113

Using the Internet

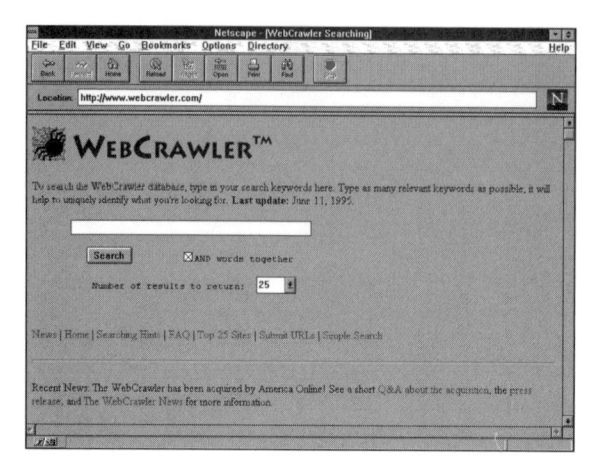

WebCrawler (http://webcrawler.com)

The WebCrawler is also one of the best general pages on the Web. It's just a search engine—a text box in which you enter your search terms—but it almost always returns a long and useful list of matching Web pages.

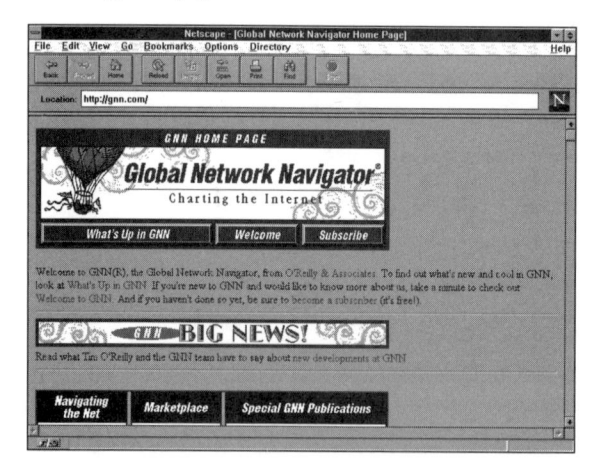

GNN (http://gnn.com)

Another good general site on the Web is Global Network Navigator (GNN), established by O'Reilly & Associates and now owned by America Online. GNN provides some information about the Internet itself, although MecklerWeb's iWorld, also described in this section, is the best source for that. You'll also find online magazines on GNN, with articles covering everything from finance to sports, plus a connection to a Web-based shopping mall.

Chapter 9: The World-Wide Web

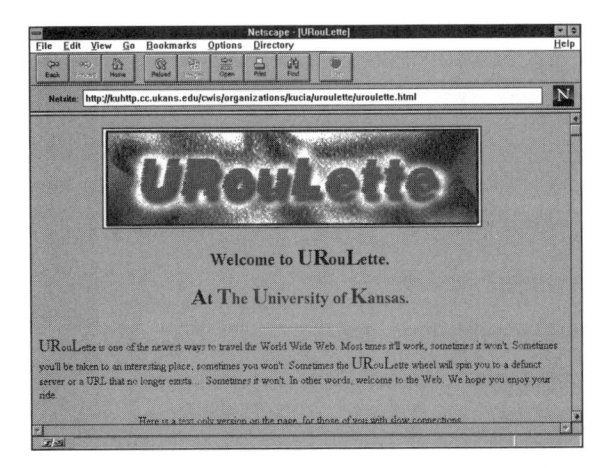

URouLette (http://kuhttp.cc.ukans.edu/cwis/organizations/kucia/uroulette/uroulette.html)

If you don't have a particular Web page in mind, try URouLette. When you select the URouLette wheel, you're sent to a random page somewhere on the Web. There are no guarantees about where you'll end up, so it's a great place to start surfing the Net.

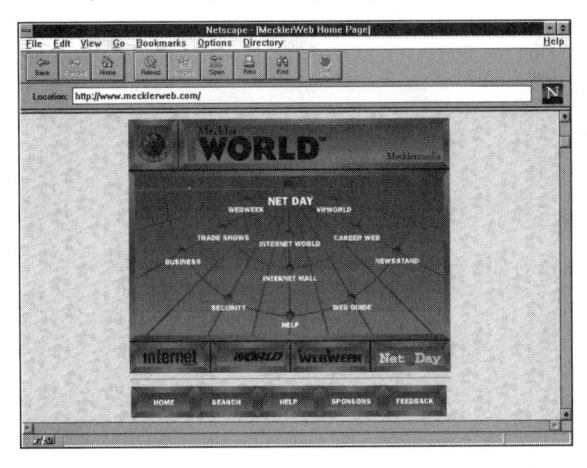

iWorld (http://www.mecklerweb.com)

If you're interested in the Internet itself, there's no better site than MecklerWeb's iWorld. Along with the full text of *Internet World* and *WebWeek* magazines, you'll find an Internet news feed, daily updates on what's hot and not on the Net, plus information about where to learn more about the Internet.

Using the Internet

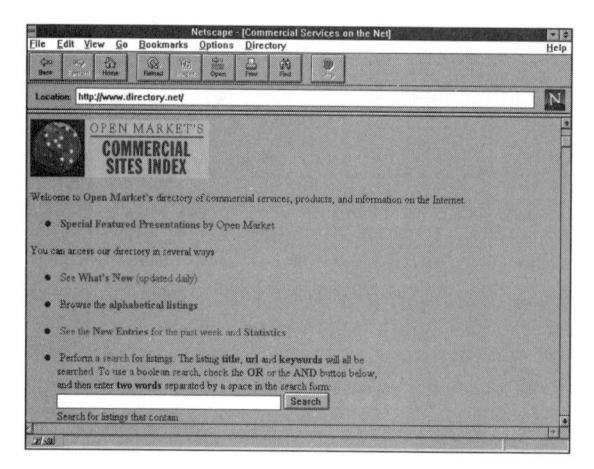

OpenMarket (http://www.directory.net)
With so many places now where you can buy things on the Internet—shoes, plants, pizza, and even underwear—OpenMarket serves as a "mall of malls," with a search tool and connections to lots of shopping areas online.

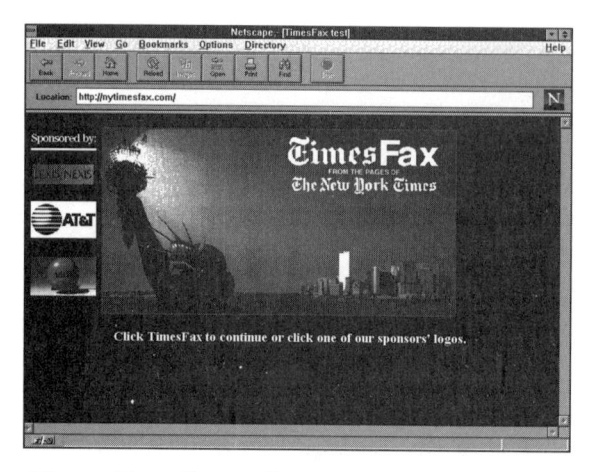

TimesFax (http://nytimesfax.com)
You can get the special Internet edition of *The New York Times* on the Web, at TimesFax. Using the downloadable Adobe Acrobat software, you can print out the eight-page paper (including the crossword puzzle) for a daily dose of what's new.

Chapter 9: The World-Wide Web

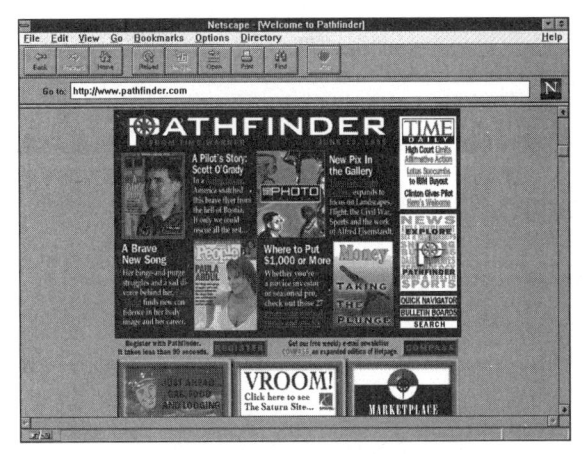

Pathfinder (http://www.pathfinder.com)

Time, Inc.'s Internet magazine has daily news from *Time* magazine, plus articles from *People* and *Entertainment Weekly*. There are also stories from *Sports Illustrated* and articles from *Fortune*, *Money*, and *Vibe*. Pathfinder is a great and successful experiment in electronic publishing, but you'll need a graphical browser.

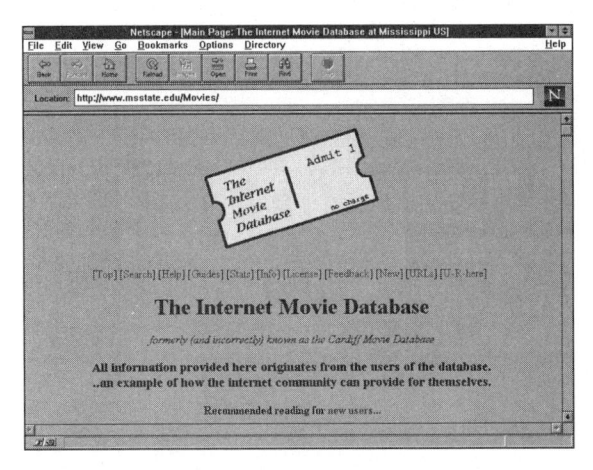

Internet Movie Database (http://www.msstate.edu/Movies)

If you like the movies, you'll love the Internet Movie Database. Here you can search for your favorite films, actors, writers, and directors. Find out what else they've done, who starred in what, and even get synopses of many motion pictures.

Surfer's Diary: Interesting and Useful Web Pages

URL	Description
http://www.opentext.com	Great Web search tool
http://www.secapl.com	Lots of stock & financial info.

Surfer's Diary: Interesting and Useful Web Pages

URL	Description

part three

moving ahead

*i*n Parts One and Two, I've given you a toolkit and shown you how to use each tool. But knowing how to use a hammer and screwdriver doesn't mean you know how to build a bookshelf or go-cart.

The first thing you need to do with your Internet toolkit is get up to speed on the individual tools.

CHAPTER TEN

getting
good

here is a review of what you need to know and what you need to do, to use those tools.

E-Mail

Electronic mail is the most popular service on the Net and it's the first thing to get up to speed on. You should know your e-mail address; if you don't, ask your system administrator. Examples are

```
ak@panix.com
tmazaro@emoryu1.cc.emory.edu
kbaxter%marketing@mail.bigcorp.com
```

Moving Ahead

Practice sending a message to a friend's e-mail address, or send a note to Bill Clinton at **president@whitehouse.gov**. You can even send a message to yourself. The point is to get familiar with your system's mailer, whether it's Pine, Elm, Eudora, or any other program.

You may also want to subscribe to some mailing lists; see Chapter 4 to learn how. Then send a message to the appropriate address and join up. Once you're comfortable reading the incoming messages, send one to the list and join in the conversation.

You know you're proficient with e-mail when you can do the following:

- Send a message to one recipient and to several recipients.
- Read messages and delete them or put them in folders.
- Reply to the sender of a message and quote the original text in your reply.
- Forward a message to someone else, adding a comment to the beginning.
- Subscribe and unsubscribe to a mailing list.

Usenet News

Once you have the basics of mailing down pat, you can move on to the next most frequented method of communicating on the Internet: Usenet News. Both Unix-based and graphical newsreaders need some practice to use properly, so it pays to spend some time learning them.

First, check out the list of available newsgroups—either by looking at your .newsrc file (Unix-based newsreaders) or by choosing Get All Newsgroups or a similar command (graphical newsreaders). Pick four or five groups that sound interesting and subscribe to them. You probably won't want to subscribe to more than a few until you're more comfortable.

Once you pick your newsgroups, start your newsreader. Most newsreaders allow you to mark all the old news items as "read," sometimes called *catching up*. Do this the first time you use Usenet News and if you've been away for a while; it will save you the trouble of facing and sorting through several hundred messages in each group. Whether or not you are allowed to do catch-up, browse through the groups you've subscribed to, marking the messages and threads (groups of messages on the same topic) you want to read.

If you want to try writing your own messages, first post to one of the test groups such as **alt.test** or **misc.test**. If you're successful, you'll receive automatic e-mail from around the world from computers that read your message. Before you post to a real newsgroup—either to reply to a message or to start a new topic—read the Netiquette section in Chapter 5. Internet users can be prickly and vocal ("That belongs in alt.kittens, not alt.cats, you moron!") so take the time to learn the culture.

You know you're proficient with Usenet News when you can do the following:

- Subscribe to a new newsgroup and mark all the old posts as "read" (so you don't have to read a thousand old posts).
- Read selected posts in a group.
- Answer ("reply") to a post via e-mail.
- Reply ("follow-up") to a post in the newsgroup and include text from the original post.
- E-mail the post to someone else.
- Save the text of a post in a file.
- Unsubscribe from a newsgroup.

P.S. You know you're *really* proficient with Usenet News when you can select and decode a multipart binary post.

IRC

Internet Relay Chat (IRC) is fairly simple to use and a good thing to know in case you want to take a break once in a while. Start 'er up and connect to a chat server. (If you're using a graphical client, you'll have to choose a server; it's automatic with Unix-based clients.) Then choose a channel—**#hottub** is a good choice, as is **#irchelp**—and listen in for a bit. When you're comfortable, say "Hello" and see what happens.

Moving Ahead

You'll also want to practice sending private messages to someone, in case you want to "whisper."

You know you're proficient with IRC when you can do the following:

- Start your IRC client and connect to a server.
- Choose or change your nickname.
- Get a list of channels.
- Join a channel.
- Send a message to the others on the channel.
- Send a private message to someone else on IRC.

Gopher

Gopher is so simple, everyone should know how to use it. Start it by typing the word **gopher** at your command prompt, or clicking on the Gopher icon if your interface is graphical. Then, using your mouse or keyboard, pick something interesting from the first menu you see. (If you're using a text-based version, the choices that lead to more choices end in a slash; choices that are readable files end with a period.) Learn how to go forward and back in the menus, and, of course, how to quit. You'll also want to save some of the information you find and practice mailing it to other people (or yourself).

You know you're proficient with Gopher when you can do the following:

- Start Gopher at the server of your choice.
- Go deeper into a menu, and go back.
- Save the text of an item in a file.
- E-mail the text of an item to someone.
- Find Veronica and search for something successfully.
- Save a Gopher location as a bookmark.
- Go back to a bookmark you've created.

The World-Wide Web

Like Gopher, the Web is a fairly simple system to use. Start up your Web browser and begin exploring from wherever

Chapter 10: Getting Good

it puts you. Then pick a page from the list in Chapter 9 and check it out. You'll also probably want to change your default startup page to something more general, such as Yahoo or the WebCrawler. Beyond that, the Web is easy—surf around, add cool pages to your hotlist, and enjoy.

You know you're proficient with the Web when you can do the following:

- Tell your browser to go to a specific page.
- Go back to a previous page.
- Save the location of a page to your hotlist.
- Go to a location on your hotlist.

CHAPTER ELEVEN

gaining
perspective

despite what Andre Agassi might say, image isn't everything. *Perspective* is everything. Sometimes all it takes to understand something is looking at it from another angle. Haven't we all said "Ah! Now I get it!" when someone gives us a little perspective? I've tried to give you a little perspective about the Internet, but it's always good to have more. That's what this chapter is about.

The mass media haven't exactly given us a very good explanation about the Internet, choosing to focus on such topics as sex and terrorism on the Net, rather than on more productive uses. Interview some average people on the street and you're likely to find a lot of folks who think the Net is a hangout for terrorists and pedophiles. (This, as anyone who has spent time

Moving Ahead

on the Net knows, is simpy not the case ... unless you're *A Current Affair* or *Time* magazine.)

There are other misconceptions floating around out there, some perpetuated by the media, and some simply the stuff of myth. The publisher wanted me to write a bigger book—against my wishes!—so I'm going to talk about some of those misconceptions and try to debunk the myths.

Another good way to get some perspective is to watch someone else. So I'll end the chapter with the tale of a "typical" Internet user and how she uses the Internet during one day of her life.

Common Misconceptions

When you get familiar with the Internet, you begin to hear some of the same questions asked and the same misconceived answers given. From newcomers to an executive editor of *PC Magazine*, people often hear, believe, or say something about the Net that just isn't so or is at least a bit off the mark. Following are some of the more common mistakes, fictions, and legends.

Isn't the Internet run by the government?

The short and easy answer is No. As described in Chapter 1, the U.S. government has until recently played a major role in the development of the Internet, but the government is not "in charge" of the Net. The government created the Internet (as ARPAnet) and started it on its way in 1969. But—although it was the largest part of the Internet—the ARPAnet wasn't the *entire* Internet. Other organizations not related to the government also used ARPAnet's technology. And by the mid-1980s the government was only one organization of many.

But the government did fund the National Science Foundation (NSF) and the NSF backbone—the Net's single largest connection. The NSF created the infamous Acceptable Use Policy or AUP, which said that no one could use the NSF's network for commercial purposes. But commercial traffic still existed on the Net, routed around the

NSF's portion of the network. In the early 1990s the NSF stopped enforcing the AUP, and commercial traffic exploded ... as did the Internet. And finally, in early 1995, the government pulled the plug on the NSFnet altogether and got out of the Internet business completely.

Isn't the Internet a large computer near Alexandria, Virginia?

Every now and then, some newspaper or magazine will run an article about how someone has "broken into" the Internet and wreaked some form of havoc or other. These articles generally give the impression that the Internet is one giant computer somewhere, and that these "hackers" have found a way into it.

That's just not the case. Unfortunately, when uninformed journalists cover a complex topic, they usually get it wrong.

Saying that someone "broke into" the Internet is like saying someone "broke into" the telephone system. First of all, there's no single thing to break into. (Where is "the telephone system"? It's not in any one place, although there are central switches and other important locations.) It also doesn't make sense because everyone has access to the Internet, just like anyone with a phone has access to the phone system. There's no *need* to break in.

What these reports usually translate into is that some nefarious soul has broken into one of the *computers* that happens to be connected to the Internet, and they probably got to that computer *through* the Net.

The Internet is not in one central place, or even in a few dozen places. It's composed of millions of separate computers around the world. They are all equal—or almost equal—components. When you connect to the Internet, you aren't connecting to a central computer; you are connecting to a system of computers, and you can then get information from all of them.

Don't pornographic images make up most of the Internet?

If you listen to too much *60 Minutes* or read *Time* magazine, that's what you may think. But it's not so. A recent

Moving Ahead

study on pornography showed that less than one percent of the information on the Internet is "dirty." That doesn't mean pornography isn't out there—of course it is—but it certainly isn't as easy to find as the mass media would have you think. And (again, despite what you might hear) it isn't always easy to view the images that *are* out there. Pornography is far more readily available in your local bookstore than on the Internet—just walk over to the magazine rack!

Sure, you might stumble across a page on the World-Wide Web with pictures of naked people, but that's not likely. First and most importantly, these pages are usually carefully labeled, so when you click on a link marked "Suzie's Sex Shop," you shouldn't be surprised at what you see. Second, no Internet access provider that hosts Web pages wants to get complaints about pornography—especially if there's no warning about it.

Images posted to Usenet newsgroups, unlike those on the Web, are not easily visible. They must be decoded first (see Chapter 5). That may require you to type in some arcane commands, or at least wait a few minutes for the images to be processed. Either way, the only way to get them is to explicitly (no pun intended) ask for them.

So, you may ask, especially if you're a parent (or a politician up for reelection), how do we protect the children? How do you keep your 10-year-old from stumbling across "Debbie Does Usenet"? There are a few ways. First, obviously, is to supervise your kids. Sending them onto the Net is like sending them into a big city. You don't just put them on a bus with some pocket money and hope for the best. At first, you go with them, learning the terrain. Then you explain where they're allowed to go and where they aren't. Finally, you may want to get some of the new software that allows parents to "block out" sites they don't want their kids to visit, like **http://www.playboy.com**. Some of these products are Cybersitter, SurfWatch, and Crossing Guard.

Isn't it illegal to advertise on the Internet?

Another short and easy answer: No. The same laws that apply to any form of expression apply to the Net. That

Chapter 11: Gaining Perspective

means it's not illegal to advertise on the Net, any more than it's illegal to advertise in a newspaper or on a billboard.

Why do people think it's illegal? Once upon a time, the National Science Foundation (NSF) ran the largest segment of the Internet, and—because it was government funded—prohibited all commercial traffic on the NSFnet. Back then, advertising *was* prohibited on a large chunk of the Net. But the government and NSF are out of the Internet business, and the restrictions on commercial traffic are gone.

On the other hand, the Internet and Usenet communities don't always take kindly to advertising, especially when it's unsolicited, off-topic, and blatant. It's probably all right to mention your mail-order bicycle shop in the **rec.bicycling** newsgroup (if you're subtle and friendly about it), but it's *not* okay to post an ad in several dozen groups. And it would be considered bad form—although, admittedly, not illegal—to send e-mail to a newsgroup's participants just because you consider them potential customers. You're likely to get a lot of nasty responses, a complaint sent to your access provider, or worse. (And take cover if you give out your phone or fax number, that's for sure!)

On the World-Wide Web, it's another story. Because people only get to Web sites voluntarily, the Web is considered a free-for-all when it comes to advertising. Companies large and small have pages on the Web, where they not only extol the virtues of whatever they're selling but will sell it to you as well. Most people who want to advertise on the Net do it the right way: They create a Web site with all the information they want to provide, and then carefully and subtly advertise the Web site in the appropriate newsgroups (and, I can tell you, also by sending press releases to *Internet World* magazine). Then they let word-of-mouth take its course.

Isn't it unsafe to send my credit card number over the Net?

I always get a kick out of people who are wary of typing their credit card number in an e-mail message. Many of these same people wouldn't think twice about giving their card number over the telephone to buy flowers or order

Moving Ahead

from a catalog. And they certainly wouldn't worry about paying a restaurant check with their card. But the chances of someone stealing your credit card number are as great—if not greater—in either of those situations than if you send it in an electronic message.

Think about it: When you give your number over the phone to an operator at L.L. Bean, for instance, you don't know who you're talking to. Nor can you be sure that someone else isn't listening in. How many times have you overheard other conversations while on the telephone? How do you know that isn't happening to you when you're on the phone to Tracy at Time-Life? And the problem is compounded if you use a cordless or cellular phone, which anyone with a police scanner might be able to tap into.

But let's say you're the type who doesn't give out your credit card number over the phone. Is there any way to give your number over the Internet and not have to worry? Absolutely.

If you want to send sensitive information over the Net, you need to encrypt it. That means you convert your easily readable information into something that's encoded, so only the people you want to can read it. A lot of people use encryption on the Internet; by far the most popular piece of software for doing this is called PGP (Pretty Good Privacy). It's available on the Internet, and the best place to find out more is in the Usenet newsgroup **alt.security.pgp**.

Besides PGP for e-mail and other electronic messages, companies that offer to sell things over the World-Wide Web use *secure servers*—meaning that their computer and your computer can communicate securely; you can send your credit card number to the merchant over the Net without fear of anyone tampering with or intercepting it.

Note: Keep in mind that you must be sure you are sending your number to a secure server; most merchants who use them will announce it. Also be sure your Web browser, as well, supports secure servers. Netscape, Spry Mosaic, and others do—and they make a point of telling you.

Chapter 11: Gaining Perspective

Isn't e-mail free?

Not exactly, any more than "all-you-can-eat" chicken wings are free at your local restaurant. When you pay for your Internet connection, you are paying for your use of the Internet, whether you use it to send one e-mail message or a hundred. The same is true of your Internet provider, who is paying another, larger provider a per-month fee for all *their* users (including you).

Many people think e-mail is free because they don't pay per message; they pay per month. (A *PC Magazine* executive editor once wrote an entire column complaining about free e-mail!) We're all accustomed to paying every time we do something—ride a bus, make a phone call, mail a letter—so we often think that if we're not paying for each use, what we're doing is free.

Wouldn't it be nice if you paid a flat monthly bill for telephone usage, and could make all the local and long-distance calls you wanted to? Send a note to your local phone company and suggest it. (But don't hold your breath.)

Isn't it a long-distance call to get information from Sweden?

This question is the evil twin of the previous one. The answer is No. Many people are afraid that because their modem is connected to the telephone line, when they retrieve information from a computer they are actually paying for a call to wherever that other computer resides. That's not the case.

When you connect to the Internet, you are connecting to your access provider's computer, and you pay for what is hopefully a local phone call (unless there's no local provider). But that is the only phone cost you pay to access the Internet. When you retrieve information from Sweden or send a message there, your provider connects to another computer nearby. That computer connects to another, and so on, until you are connected by a long chain to your target computer in Stockholm. *But you only pay for your local phone call!* Who pays for the rest? The cost is distributed among the various computers and networks that are

Moving Ahead

between you and Sweden; each pays to maintain a segment of the entire connection.

You pay your Internet provider, and so do a lot of other users. Your provider uses that money to pay for its connection to the rest of the Net. So the cost of the Internet is distributed, and you don't have to pay for a long-distance call to Europe.

Aren't viruses a problem? Can't you get one from e-mail?

Viruses, in case you didn't know, are computer programs that are designed to hide in your computer while "attached" to another program. Viruses are usually bad programs—they are written to do nasty things to your computer, like erase your hard drive, alter your data, and other similar nightmares. Computer viruses are able to copy themselves from one program to another, and from one computer to another; if you get a program that has a virus, you will eventually find your entire hard drive infected. And if you give a copy of an infected program to someone else, their computer will become infected as well. That's how viruses spread.

Naturally, because the Internet makes transferring information—including computer programs—so easy, people are afraid that they may catch a virus.

There's good news and bad news on this score. The bad news is yes, you might very well encounter a virus on the Internet.

The good news comes in several parts. First of all, viruses aren't as common as many people—including the mass media—would have you believe. They're out there, but they aren't lurking behind every FTP site. Second, virus-detection and -killing software is plentiful, and in many cases free. (Check out the **comp.virus** newsgroup for more information.) The software is easy to use; you simply inspect any software you download from the Net, *before* you run the software.

That leads to the rest of the good news. Viruses can only be carried by programs, not by data. If you get a copy of the complete works of Shakespeare, for instance, it cannot possibly contain a virus—it's just data. On the other hand (or OTOH, in Netspeak), when you get a copy of a game or a screen-saver program, a virus could be attached. That's why you should run a virus checker before you use that acquired program. You cannot get a virus from e-mail—unless that e-mail has a program attached to it. In that case your e-mail software will alert you to that fact with a message such as "Attachment COOLGAME.EXE converted to C:\TEMP\COOLGAME.EXE." So you run your virus checker on the file *before* you run the game.

Avoiding viruses is just a matter of a little knowledge and common sense.

Doesn't everyone hate newbies on the Internet?

Yes. (But how will anyone know you're a newbie unless you act like one?)

Isn't there a directory of everyone's address on the Internet?

I wish there were—I wouldn't get nearly as many phone calls as I do. There are no Internet White Pages, for a very simple reason: There are too many people online in too many places. It's like asking for a White Pages for the world. Besides the fact that there are over 12 million people on the Net, those people are at separate locations. So you'd need to get a list of all the people at every school, college, university, research institution, government office, and corporation that's connected. That's one big list.

People often ask what's the best way to find someone's e-mail address. The answer is still the same: Ask. Why? Imagine you meet someone on an airplane flight to Europe. He tells you his name is Richard Kimball, but that's it. How will you find his phone number? You could look in a phone book, but which one? If he's North American, you have 50 states and a dozen Canadian provinces to look at—that's a lot of phone books! In the same way, just knowing that someone is on the Internet doesn't mean you know what computer he or she connects through. But, if you know the name of his provider, you stand a much better chance of finding Mr. Kimball.

Occasionally, you'll see books that claim to be a "White Pages for the Internet"; you may even find such a service online. Although they probably have a lot of addresses listed, I would bet that many of them are outdated (one such book listed an address for me that I had in college!). And, of course, any printed list of addresses is quickly outdated, as thousands of people connect to the Internet every month.

If you can get files from other computers, can other people get into your hard drive?

Nope. Not a chance. In order for a person (or organization) to allow outsiders to get information from their computer, the person (or organization) would have to install special software—server software—that will allow it. Without that software, there is no way for their computer to understand requests from other computers. You can't get blood from a stone; you can't get files without a server.

A Day in the Life

Sometimes the best way to see how someone uses the Internet is to follow that person around. There are two ways to do this: Find a friend who spends a lot of time online and watch over his or her shoulder for a few hours, or read this section.

Let's follow Kirsten, a (presumably) fictional Internet user, through a day of using the Net. Kirsten is not quite a power user, but she uses the Net more than an average person, which is perfect for this example. (Note: The products mentioned in this example are fictional.)

When Kirsten wakes up, she turns on her computer and starts her e-mail program. Then she takes a shower and gets dressed. She has set her e-mail software so it dials into her Internet access provider, downloads her waiting e-mail, and then disconnects so she doesn't spend too much time on the phone.

Before she leaves for work, she reads her mail. She's received nine new messages overnight: three from other participants in her photography mailing list (she subscribed

Chapter 11: Gaining Perspective

a few months ago); two from friends (one local and one 2,000 miles away); two from her electronic news "droid," which searches various news services for articles containing the name of her company or the name of the stock she owns; and two from her boyfriend (a joke that's being circulated around the Net, and a suggestion for a place to go for dinner that evening). Because none of the messages are urgent, Kirsten shuts down her computer and goes to work.

Kirsten's office is not quite on the cutting edge of technology, so she doesn't have a full Internet connection from her desktop computer there. She can, however, exchange electronic mail with the Net. Kirsten keeps her office mail separate from home, so—after a cup of coffee and a bagel (onion, with cream cheese)—she starts up her office e-mail.

There she finds over a dozen messages. Most of them are from within her office: mail from people she works with discussing everything from the new furniture in the lunchroom to the new marketing plan. Some of the mail she reads and deletes because it doesn't interest her; some she files in various mail folders to keep or look at later; and some she replies to right away.

During her day at work, Kirsten exchanges a few e-mail messages with people on the Net. Her boyfriend drops another note about dinner, and over the course of an hour they decide to go to that restaurant the next day.

She also receives a message from Kara, a college friend who works in another state—it's a copy of the Top-Ten list from last night's Letterman show. Kirsten likes getting the list every day, so she finally takes the time to sign up for it herself. To **listserv@listserv.clark.net** she sends a note that consists of the line **subscribe topten Kirsten Baxter**. A few minutes later she receives a confirmation that she'll receive the list every day. (It's free, of course, and she knows this for a very simple reason: She was never asked to pay.)

Throughout her work day, Kirsten sends and receives a variety of e-mail messages, some work related and some personal. At about 5:30, she goes home.

Kirsten has signed up with a local Internet access provider because she wants to keep her work e-mail and her personal messages separate. She also wants access to

Moving Ahead

the things she can't get at work, specifically Usenet News and the World-Wide Web. After dinner (and before *Mad About You* starts), she sits down to catch up on things.

First, as always, she checks her e-mail. A few more messages have come in, one of which tells her that some stock she bought last year (against her boyfriend's advice) is up again. She forwards the report to him with a note on top that reads "I told you so!" Her news service sends her a list of top science news stories; one is about a planned probe to Saturn. Kirsten decides to read more about it, so she sends a note to the news service asking for the detailed report.

That full story will take about five minutes to be processed, so she leaves her e-mail program and goes to Usenet News. Kirsten enjoys photography, and she follows the **rec.photo.darkroom** and **rec.photo.help** newsgroups among others. She's been involved with a discussion about a new kind of black-and-white film from Kodak. Several people, including Kirsten, have tried the film and they are comparing notes. One of the posts mentions that Kodak has supplied darkroom information about the file on their World-Wide Web site. Kirsten makes a note of the address.

She also finds that someone has replied to a post of hers in a bicycling newsgroup, in which she asked for suggestions for a toolkit to take on a long trip. Two people replied, both recommending the same product (BikeBox, made by a company called Bike Stuff Inc.). She thanks them for their help and shuts down her newsreader.

Lastly, Kirsten starts her Web browser, first going to the Kodak page and working her way through the links there until she finds darkroom information about the new film. Once she finds the right page, rather than copy it down on paper, she simply instructs her browser to save it to her hard disk so she can print it later.

Then she decides to see if Bike Stuff has a page on the Web. She goes to Yahoo (**http://www.yahoo.com**) and does a search on Bicycle. From a list of over 60 companies, she finds Bike Stuff and goes to their home page. It isn't the fanciest page she's ever seen, but it does link to a catalog of

Chapter 11: Gaining Perspective

all their products—including BikeBox (suggested retail price $39.95). Unfortunately, Bike Stuff won't let her order it through their Web site, but that's all right; Kirsten figures she can get it for less at a local store. She notices that the company has a searchable list of stores that sell Bike Stuff products, so she enters her zip code. A moment later she gets a list of three stores near her. She copies down their names and phone numbers, shuts down her browser, and disconnects from the Net.

All in a day's work.

CHAPTER TWELVE

useful resources

his is a beginner's book, and one you're sure to outgrow in time. There are many other sources of information out there, and choosing which ones to buy can be an exercise in futility. I've narrowed the field considerably; here are the three best printed resources for the Internet novice.

Internet World. The best ongoing source of Internet-related information is *Internet World* magazine, and I don't say that just because I'm the senior editor there. It's designed for newcomers to the Net, companies looking Net-ward, and long-time users who want to get the most out of their online time. There are news, announcements, and hints, plus feature articles, interviews, book reviews, and other useful information. *Internet*

Moving Ahead

World is published monthly and is available on newsstands, in bookstores, and by subscription. Call (800) 573-3062 or send e-mail to **subs@mecklermedia.com** for information.

The Internet For Dummies. This #1 best-selling Internet reference helps you cruise the net with ease. Published by IDG Books Worldwide, *The Internet For Dummies* sells for $19.99.

The Internet Complete Reference. When it comes to learning the ins and outs and the nitty-gritty of the Net, this book you're reading will get you started, but it's hard to beat Harley Hahn and Rick Stout's 800+ page reference. *The Internet Complete Reference* is published by Osborne/McGraw-Hill and sells for $29.95.

Your Internet Consultant. Kevin Savetz has written the other "best" Internet reference. *Your Internet Consultant: The FAQs of Life Online* answers all your how-to questions about the Net—everything from finding files to sending faxes. It sells for $25.00 and is published by Sams Publishing.

a final note

Congratulations—you made it through. You now have a better understanding of this Internet thing, and will be able to get online—to "jack in, log on, and geek out," as it were. It's worth it.

You can make a lot of analogies about the Internet. It's a government experiment gone awry. It's a giant electronic flea market. It's a successful experiment in anarchy. It's just a lot of computers.

All of these are true.

In the end, though, the Internet is just there. It's what you make of it: an information resource, a place to meet friends, or a tool to send messages. Like any relationship, making the Internet work for you requires that you work a bit for it. Take the time to read, to watch, and to learn. With only a small effort, you can make the Net pay off.

—Andrew Kantor

glossary

Note: The terms in this glossary are defined in terms of the Internet, specifically for new users. Some of them have more specific or even entirely different meanings in other areas of computing.

Note: The numbers in parentheses at the end of each glossary term definition indicates the chapter number where the term is discussed.

! In Unix parlance, a "bang." When seen in the .newsrc file, means that you are not subscribed to a particular newsgroup (i.e., alt.dinosaurs.barney!). Also often used to separate sections of an e-mail address. (5)

(pound sign or hash mark) A symbol preceding every IRC channel (#jeopardy and #chat, for instance). (6)

$ One of several standard Unix prompts; another popular one is the %. (3)

@ In every e-mail address, separates the username from the domain name. (4)

.newsrc In a shell account, the file that lists all the newsgroups that your Internet provider has available. (5)

.plan A file shown to any user who uses the finger command on your account. A .plan file typically contains some brief autobiographical information about its owner. (3)

Glossary

.profile A text file that contains commands your Unix account will automatically execute each time you log in. (3)

.signature A short message automatically attached to every Usenet News posting and e-mail message you send out. (3)

alias In a Unix .profile or .cshrc file, a phrase that substitutes for a longer command. (3)

alt The largest of the major hierarchies on Usenet News (short for alternative). Covers those topics that do not fall into any of the other hierarchies. (5)

Anonymous FTP *See* FTP.

Archie A program that, given a keyword, searches the Internet for a specific filename. (7)

ARPAnet A network developed in 1969 by ARPA (the Advanced Research Project Agency), and predecessor to the Internet. The *packet-switching* technology used in the ARPAnet was vital to the evolution of the Internet. (1)

attachment A nontext or binary file that accompanies an e-mail message. (4)

Berlin, Eric Author of this glossary (eric@panix.com).

binary file Any nontext file such as a graphic, piece of software, spreadsheet, sound, etc. (4)

BinHex A popular method on the Macintosh for attaching binary files to e-mail messages. MIME is more popular, but certain Macintosh packages only support BinHex. (4)

bookmark In a Gopher or World Wide Web client, a list of favorite sites. By creating bookmarks, it's easy to return to places you have visited previously. (9)

bot A software program that acts as a moderator on an IRC channel. Bots typically judge ongoing, interactive games or scold IRC users for using bad language. (6)

browser A piece of software used to travel the World Wide Web. Graphical browsers include Mosaic and Netscape. (9)

Glossary

channel A section of the IRC, analogous to a CB radio channel. Once you join an IRC channel, everything you type will be seen by everyone else on that channel. (6)

client Software required to use a certain server to retrieve various types of information on the Internet. For instance, to get information from a Gopher server, you need Gopher client software. (6)

communications software Software that allows you to control your modem. (2)

comp A Usenet News hierarchy for discussion of different types of computers and computer-related issues—for instance, **comp.graphics.misc**. (5)

dial-up access An Internet connection established over phone lines and using a modem. (2)

direct connection An Internet connection through a network, as opposed to via a modem. (2)

directory (or folder on a Mac) A location on a computer where files are found. A particular computer will always have a main or root directory, and will probably have an assortment of subdirectories. (3)

domain name The official Internet name of your provider's computer, usually something like provider.com or ppp.provider.com. (2)

dynamic IP Address used by some Internet access providers. This will give you a different IP address each time you connect to the Internet. (2)

e-mail Short for electronic mail; a method of sending individual messages to other Internet users. (4)

e-mail address The electronic address that people use to send mail to you. Examples are ak@panix.com and kara%art%marketing@mail.bigcorp.com. (4)

Elm A popular Unix e-mail program, written by Dave Taylor. (4)

149

Glossary

emoticon Also known as a "smiley," a sideways smile or other representation of a face created with standard characters. Examples are :-) and ;^).

Eudora Qualcomm's graphical e-mail program used over SLIP/PPP or direct connections. (4)

FAQ file An abbreviation for Frequently Asked Questions file. A list of popular questions and answers on a given subject. Most newsgroups have a FAQ file posted periodically for new readers of that newsgroup. It is considered polite to read through a newsgroup's FAQ file before posting to the group. (5)

finger A Unix command that allows you to see certain information about someone else on the Internet, including that person's .plan file. (3)

flame An argumentative, often insulting message. Exchanges of such messages may be referred to as "flame wars."(5)

follow-up A response to a message that is posted to the same Usenet newsgroup where it was read. In the message thread, the original message is often indicated by a bracket (>). (5)

FTP An abbreviation for File Transfer Protocol—The method of retrieving files from other computers on the Internet. (7)

Gopher On the Internet, a system of organizing information in a series of menus and submenus. Anyone with access to a Gopher client can access this information. (8)

Gopherspace Term indicating every Gopher menu on the Internet. (8)

handle A nickname used on the IRC. (6)

hierarchies The way the Usenet News community keeps its thousands of newsgroups organized. There are eight major hierarchies: alt, comp, misc, news, rec, sci, soc, and talk. Many other hierarchies exist for people in specific geographical areas. (The fj hierarchy, for instance, is for people in Japan, il for people in Israel, etc.) (5)

Glossary

home directory The place on an Internet provider's computer where you can store any files you retrieve. (3)

home page An organization's page on the World Wide Web; the one first seen by users. (9)

host name The name of a computer connected to the Internet, i.e., mecklermedia.com or whitehouse.gov. (2)

hotlist An individual user's list of frequented sites on the World Wide Web. By keeping a hotlist in your Web browser, it is easier to return to sites you visit often. (9)

hypertext Items in a computerized document that, when clicked on, take you to more detailed information on that topic. Used extensively in World Wide Web pages. (9)

Internet A giant, worldwide collection of millions of interconnected computers and computer networks. (1)

Internet access provider A company that, usually for a fee, provides a connection to the Internet for individuals and/or organizations. (2)

Internet Relay Chat *See* IRC.

internetwork A group of connected computer networks. (1)

IP address Your numerical address on the Internet (see also *domain name*). IP addresses look like the following: 123.45.65.456. You need to know your IP address only when first configuring a SLIP connection. (2)

IRC Internet Relay Chat. The Internet's version of a CB radio, with thousands of people typing online messages to one another in real time. (6)

links A method of traveling the World Wide Web using hypertext. Links on one page lead you to other pages (possibly on other computers) with related information. (9)

listserv Another term for an electronic mailing list. Allows people interested in the same subject to easily exchange e-mail. (4)

local area network (LAN) A small network, probably found within a specific geographical location. (4)

Glossary

Lynx A text-based Web browser that runs on Unix computers. (9)

mailing list *See* listserv.

MIME encoding A popular way of sending a binary file as an attachment with an e-mail message. MIME stands for Multipurpose Internet Mail Extensions. (4)

mirror An FTP site that keeps copies of files on other sites. When one computer is overloaded with requests for files, the administrators will often suggest that users get the files from mirror sites. (7)

misc A Usenet News hierarchy, short for Miscellaneous, that covers many "forsale" newsgroups and other practical discussions. (5)

modem A computer accessory that allows you to call other computers using standard phone lines. Stands for modulator/demodulator. (2)

Netiquette The unwritten, but still very real, code of rules for behavior on the Internet. (4)

netmask Also called subnet mask. Like an IP address, this is part of your addressing scheme when setting up a SLIP connection. A netmask looks like the following: 255.255.255.0. (2)

network A group of connected computers. (1)

news A Usenet News hierarchy that specifically discusses the ever-changing face of Usenet News. (5)

news server (or perhaps NNTP news server). The name of the computer that handles Usenet News. It will probably have a name like news.provider.com. (2)

newsgroup An individual discussion group on Usenet News—for instance, rec.pets.cats or alt.fan.jay-leno. (5)

newsreader software software that allows you to read Usenet News. (5)

nn Newsreader software used on a Unix shell account. Stands for "no news is good news." (5)

Glossary

NNTP server *See* news server.

online services Large organizations such as America Online, CompuServe, and Prodigy that provide communications and information services for computer users. They may also provide access to the Internet, but often at a more expensive rate than dedicated Internet access providers. (2)

packet switching Technology developed by ARPA that allows electronic messages to be delivered over a network even if some computers on that network are not functioning. (1)

page A screen of information on the World Wide Web; it may contain links to other pages. (9)

PDIAL The Public Dial-up Internet Access List. A slightly out-of-date but still useful list of Internet access providers. To get the list, send e-mail to **info-deli-server@netcom.com**. The subject line should read **send pdial**; the body of the message can be empty. (2)

Pico One of several text editors found in the Unix operating system (3)

Pine An e-mail program used on Unix shell accounts. (4)

POP account The full address that your mail will go to; it might not necessarily be your e-mail address. A user with the address ak@iw.com may have a POP account of ak@mail.iw.com. (The last part, mail.iw.com, is the mail server.) (2)

PPP A slightly improved version of SLIP. Stands for Point to Point Protocol. (2)

rec A Usenet News hierarchy for newsgroups with a recreational slant—for instance, rec.skiing. (5)

reply A response to a newsgroup message that is e-mailed directly to that message's author. (4)

sci A Usenet News hierarchy for discussion of various scientific issues—for instance, sci.med.pharmacy. (5)

Glossary

server A computer on the Internet that serves information to other computers (which run client software). For instance, there are Archie servers, World Wide Web servers, Gopher servers, etc. (2)

shell An interface for the Unix operating system. There are many different types of shells, including sh (the Bourne shell), csh (C shell), and ksh (the Korn shell). (3)

shell account The most basic type of Internet connection. With a shell account, you use your keyboard to control a computer that is connected to the Internet; your own computer hardly does any work at all. (The alternative to a shell account is a SLIP connection.) (2)

SLIP connection A way to connect your own computer directly to the Internet via a phone line, thus allowing the use of user-friendly graphical utilities (as opposed to a *shell account*). May also be called a PPP connection, PPP being a slightly improved version of SLIP. SLIP is an acronym for serial-line internetworking protocol. (2)

smiley *See* emoticon.

SMTP mail server The name of the computer that handles your e-mail; you need to know this only to configure graphical e-mail software. *See* POP account. (2)

soc A Usenet News hierarchy for discussion of various social and cultural issues—for instance, soc.culture.romania. (5)

spam The posting of a single message to dozens or hundreds or even thousands of unrelated Usenet newsgroups. A *serious* Usenet no-no. (5)

subscribe The act of choosing a specific newsgroup to follow or mailing list to receive. You can then later unsubscribe from that newsgroup or list. (5)

surfing The fine art of traversing the Internet in search of anything cool and interesting.

talk A Usenet News hierarchy for the discussion of various political and religious issues, with a smattering of social discussions thrown in. (5)

Glossary

telnet A Unix procedure that allows you to connect and log on to another computer on the Internet. (3)

thread An individual discussion (including the original message and all of its follow-ups) in a particular newsgroup. (5)

tin Newsreader software used on a Unix shell account. (5)

trn Newsreader software used on a Unix shell account. Stands for "threaded read news." (5)

troll A slang term for posting messages to a newsgroup designed to annoy others there and start a *flame* war; for instance, posting a pro-Greenpeace message in **alt.fan.rush-limbaugh**.

uniform resource locator (URL) The standard addressing format for pages on the World Wide Web and other Internet sites. It takes the form type://computer/directory —as in gopher://gopher.panix.com or http://www.iw.com/iw. (9)

Unix A complicated, powerful operating system used on many Internet-accessible computers. (3)

URL *See* uniform resource locator.

Usenet News The electronic bulletin board carried by the Internet (and other networks), on which approximately 15,000 different newsgroups carry discussions on millions of topics. (5)

UUencoding One process by which binary files such as pictures, spreadsheets, and programs are converted to text files, in order to be more easily e-mailed. *See also* MIME and BinHex. (4)

Veronica An Internet tool that searches Gopherspace for a particular piece of information. (5)

wide area network (WAN) A collection of connected computers that extend beyond a small geographic location. A company with offices in New York, Chicago, and San Jose would use a wide area network to connect all its computers. *See also* local area network.

Glossary

World-Wide Web Often abbreviated to simply "the Web" or "WWW." An Internet hypermedia menu system in which pages of information can contain pictures, text, and links to other pages. (9)

APPENDIX

guide to included software

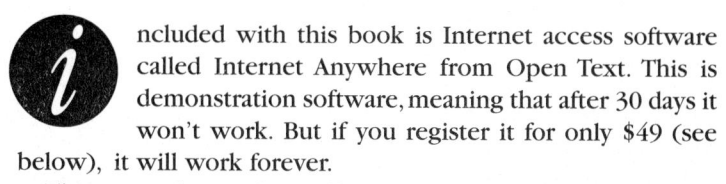

*i*ncluded with this book is Internet access software called Internet Anywhere from Open Text. This is demonstration software, meaning that after 30 days it won't work. But if you register it for only $49 (see below), it will work forever.

This appendix explains all you need to know to start using Internet Anywhere. If you have any questions about installing the software, it has an extensive online help facility.

Appendix

Open Text Internet Anywhere Demonstration

Open Text Internet Anywhere software included with this book lets you surf the World-Wide Web using the Enhanced Mosaic Web browser.

This demonstration software is operational for 30 days from the time of installation. When the 30 days is over, the software will no longer work, until you upgrade to the full version of Open Text Internet Anywhere.

Upgrading to the Full Version

Open Text offers users of this demonstration software a special upgrade price of $49.00 U.S. To upgrade your software, contact Open Text by phone, fax, or e-mail:

Phone: (800) 507-5777 or (519) 888-9910
Fax: (519) 888-0677
E-mail: iasales@opentext.com

To receive the special upgrade price be sure to mention that you are an owner of *Internet World 60 Minute Guide to the Internet Including the World-Wide Web*. When you upgrade your software, Open Text will send the full version to you via mail. Technical support will be provided when you upgrade to the full version.

Note: Please read the installation section in its entirety prior to beginning your installation session.

Installing the Open Text Internet Anywhere Demonstration Software

This section contains instructions for installing Open Text Internet Anywhere and configuring your system to communicate to an Internet access provider. You must install the software on your hard drive.

Appendix: Guide to Included Software

Note: Due to the nature of the Internet itself, you need a SLIP/PPP account with an Internet access provider before you can connect. Open Text Internet Anywhere includes an automatic account at a pre-configured access provider offering 30 days or 5 hours of free Internet access. Or you can select any access provider of your choice.

Step 1: Installation

The Setup program, included on the Internet Anywhere CD-ROM copies all of the necessary files onto your computer's hard disk.

To avoid any conflicts between the Setup program and other programs running on your computer, shut down any programs you are currently running under Windows (except Windows itself, of course). Then run the Setup program:

1. Place the installation CD in the CD-ROM drive.
2. Select the **Run** command from the Windows Program Manager's File menu. This prompts you to enter a command line.
3. Type in the path and file name of the Internet Anywhere Setup program. Click **OK**, and the Setup program begins. After it initializes, you see a dialog box asking you to enter the directory where you want to install Internet Anywhere.
4. Click on the **OK** button to accept the default installation directory. (Or type in a different drive and directory name, if desired.)
5. Click on the **OK** button to begin copying files.
   The Setup program will automatically copy all of the necessary files onto your hard drive in the directory you specified.

Once you have the files installed on your computer, you need to configure a connection with an Internet access provider. In fact, the Setup program automatically starts the

Appendix

configuration process upon completion. Step 2 explains the access provider that comes with Internet Anywhere, or tells you how to obtain a connection with another access provider if you so choose. Step 3 provides instructions for initially configuring your connection with an access provider.

Step 2 (Optional): Connection to Access Provider

An access provider is a company or organization that provides you with an electronic connection to the Internet. The Internet is not just out there for you to begin using. You need to connect with someone who is already connected to the Internet, and your access provider is that link.

The best way to describe an access provider is to think of it as a "gateway." You establish a connection to an access provider to enter the Internet, and you leave the Internet by ending that connection. In fact, the term *gateway* is commonly used to describe the computers that serve your Internet requests.

The standard service for connecting to the Internet is TCP/IP, which stands for Transmission Control Protocol/Internet Protocol. TCP/IP is the set of signals your modem sends to make it understandable by all other computers using the same protocol. To use Internet Anywhere, you need an account with an access provider who supplies TCP/IP service using SLIP (Serial Line Internet Protocol) or PPP (Point to Point Protocol).

Internet Anywhere's Preconfigured Access Provider

Open Text Internet Anywhere includes an automatic account at a preconfigured access provider. Portal Information Network, one of the largest access providers in North America, offers users of Internet Anywhere a TCP/IP account with 30 days or 5 hours of free Internet access, from more than 1,600 local access numbers.

If you choose to use the preconfigured access provider, Internet Anywhere automatically creates a TCP/IP account for you at Portal Information Network. To learn how to get

Appendix: Guide to Included Software

your automatic account, skip the rest of this section and proceed to Step 3.

Using a Different Access Provider

Arranging a connection to a specific access provider usually involves making a telephone call to the provider and asking for a PPP account. After answering a few questions about your system and requirements, the provider gives you the information you need to configure your account—login name, password, and so on.

Once you know the provider satisfies your requirements and you decide to use their services, you need to know a few details about your account.

Often the provider will send you all of the account details by fax or postal mail. But many times the account details are given to you over the phone, so you need to make sure you get all of the necessary information. We recommend that you obtain the following details; you will need to reference them when you configure your connection with Internet Anywhere.

- Your Internet *domain name*
- Your *login ID* (aka *username*)
- Your *password*
- The provider's *dial-up phone (modem) number*
- The *default gateway/IP router* IP address or domain name
- The *host/peer* IP address
- The *subnet mask*
- The *login script* (send/expect sequence)
- The supported modem *baud rates*
- The *parity*, *data bits* and *stop bits* of the provider's modem

Step 3: Configuration

When the Setup program finishes, the configuration process—also known as the *First-Time Personalization* process—automatically begins. This takes you through each

Appendix

configuration step. You must supply details about your computer and your connection to an Internet access provider.

During First-Time Personalization, you are given the choice of using Internet Anywhere's preconfigured access provider, Portal Information Network, or manually configuring a different access provider. If you choose to accept an automatic account with the preconfigured access provider, most of the First-Time Personalization process is completed for you.

Regardless of the access provider you choose, you must fill in the details in each dialog box presented during First-Time Personalization, based on information about your system. If you are manually configuring a different access provider, be sure to fill in the information you have received from that provider.

If you need additional information about any step of the First Time Personalization process, press the F1 key for help.

When the First-Time Personalization process is complete, you are ready to go. Double-click on the Internet Anywhere program icon, and your Internet journey begins.

Note: Every step of the personalization process must be completed in order to connect to the Internet.

The Enhanced Mosaic Web Browser

The Internet Anywhere Enhanced Mosaic Web browser makes the Internet more accessible by displaying information in hypertext pages, letting you click on a region of your screen to quickly navigate around the world, and find the information you're looking for. Information is presented through various multimedia elements such as graphics, photos, sound, and animation. Collectively, all of the computers in the world that offer these hypertext pages of information are known as the World-Wide Web (WWW).

Browsing World-Wide Web Pages

Essentially, to access any page on the World-Wide Web you simply need to supply its *address* in the entry field at the top of the window. Every page has a unique address, much

Appendix: Guide to Included Software

like a postal address, called a *Uniform Resource Locator* (or **URL**). There is one main rule when specifying these addresses: each URL must begin with the **HTTP** prefix, which stands for *HyperText Transfer Protocol*.

For example, to view the home page of IBM, you would enter their home page's URL (with the **http** prefix): **http://www.ibm.com/**.

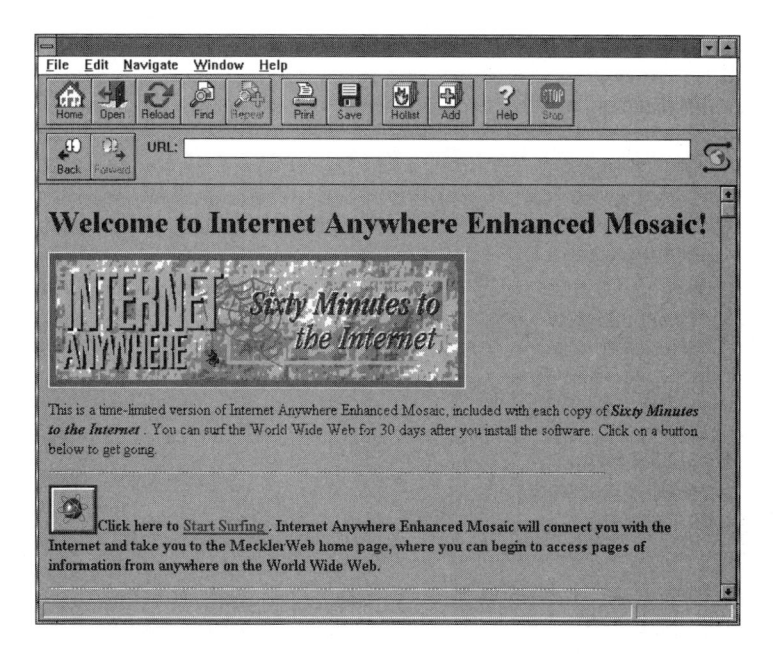

Hyperlinks

Some WWW pages contain hyperlinks that point to the URLs of other pages. In this way, browsing for related information is easy—you simply click on a region of your screen to move to a new page. For example, a page on British literature can link the word "Shakespeare" to a page listing the writer's work by title. Each title in that page could, in turn, be linked to a complete work.

Hotlists

You can save your favorite WWW page URL's in a hotlist. The hotlist is a separate window that is quickly accessible

Appendix

from the toolbar and allows you to store the addresses on the web you wish to return to at a later time.

History

Another window records the various places you have visited during your web browsing, allowing you to return to any point at any time. This comes in handy when you have wandered across the web and want to return to a specific page viewed earlier.

Usenet News and FTP

Instead of using the HyperText Transfer Protocol (**HTTP**) prefix from the Enhanced Mosaic browser, you can read Usenet newsgroups with the **NEWS** prefix, and you can download files from other computers with the **FTP** prefix.

Usenet is a collection of forums, called newsgroups, where discussion and debate on almost any topic imaginable takes place. You can read the contents of any newsgroup on Usenet by entering its name after the **NEWS** prefix. For example, if you type **news:alt.tv.simpsons** you can read articles regarding *The Simpsons* television program from people all over the world.

FTP stands for *File Transfer Protocol*. It allows you to copy a file from a computer on the Internet to your own computer. It works the same way: you just use the **FTP** prefix with the address of a computer on the Internet that offers FTP services. For example, a common FTP site offering thousands of files for downloading is Walnut Creek CD-ROM. You can view and download files there by typing the command **ftp:ftp.cdrom.com**.

Integrated Sound Player and Graphics Viewer

The Enhanced Mosaic Web browser includes a sound player that lets you play AU or AIFF sound files. If you click on a hyperlink of a sound file in one of these formats, the player automatically plays these files on your system (you need a sound card and speakers or headphones). A graphics viewer displays any files in GIF or JPEG format. It also appears auto-

Appendix: Guide to Included Software

matically upon downloading graphics files, and lets you save the files on your hard disk.

The Open Text Web Index

Available from your home page, the Open Text Web Index is a search tool that locates any term or phrase on any page of the World-Wide Web. When you supply a keyword or phrase, the search engine looks through more than a million web pages to find matches to your queries. You can perform simple, compound, or ranked searches and restrict your searches to specific structural elements of web pages, such as *title*.

To access the Open Text Web Index, just click on the **Web Index** button from within your home page (the page that appears whenever you start the browser). You can perform a simple search by typing in a word or phrase in the entry field and clicking on the **Search** button. Additional instructions and help are available from the Web Index page.

Index

<> angle brackets), 60, 66
* (asterisk), 75
: (colon), 57
$ (dollar sign), 10, 22, 29, 147
! (exclamation point), 34, 57
% (percent sign), 10, 22, 34
# (pound sign), 75, 147
+ (plus sign), 61, 75
/ (slash), 74, 81

A

addresses. See also e-mail addresses
  IP addresses, 12, 149, 151
  telnet, 30
Adobe Acrobat, 116
adoptees, mailing list for, 45
advertising
  on the Internet, legality of, 132-133
  mailing lists and, 45
  newsgroups and, 67
Agassi, Andre, 129
Air Mail (Spry), 36
aliases, 26-27, 98, 148
alt newsgroups, 54, 148
  alt.binaries.pictures newsgroup, 65
  alt.security.pgp newsgroup, 133
Alternet, 16
Amiga computers, 108
analytic philosophy mailing list, 45
angle brackets (<>), 60, 66
Anonymous FTP, 10, 164
  Archie and, 87-89, 97

167

basic description of, 18, 79-91, 150
directories and, 26
by e-mail, 83-84
getting connected to the Internet and, 18, 19
getting Eudora through, 40
IRC and, 77
mirrored sites and, 85, 152
recommended sites, 85-86
Usenet News and, 67
using, overview of, 80-83
the World Wide Web and, 104, 110-111
AOL (American Online)
basic description of, 16
e-mail, 14
GNN and, 114
software, 13, 16
arachnid mailing list, 45
Archie, 19, 29-30, 79, 81, 97, 148
basic description of, 86-89
clients, 73
servers, 86
ARPA (Advanced Research Projects Agency), 4, 153. *See also* ARPAnet
ARPAnet, 4, 130, 148
arrow keys, 37, 107, 108
ASCII text, file extension for, 84
asterisk (*), 75
at sign (@), 34, 147
attach commands, 41-42
Attach Document command, 42
Attach File command, 42
attachments, to e-mail, 41-42, 137, 148
AUP (Acceptable Use Policy), 130-131

B

Back button, 108
ballroom dancing mailing list, 46
ba newsgroups, 54
"bang," 57, 147
barbershop music mailing list, 46
BBSs (bulletin-board systems), 53-54. *See also* newsgroups; Usenet News
Berlin, Eric, 148
biblio mailing list, 46
binary files, 148, 155
posting, in newsgroups, 64-65
sending, through e-mail, 41-42
BinHex, 42, 148
biz newsgroups, 54
bookmarks, 110, 126, 148
"bots," 72, 148
Bourne shell, 26, 154
Britain, 34
browsers. *See* Web browsers

C

California, 4, 54
cancel action
in e-mail programs, 39
Unix command for, 22
Carnegie-Mellon University, 113
case-sensitivity, 81, 87
CB radio, 71
cd command, 37
Cello, 108
characters. *See* symbols
chat servers, 72
children
access of, to the Internet, 132
mailing list for, 47

Index

CICA site, 85
clari newsgroups, 54
clients
  Archie, 73
  definition of, 73, 149
  Gopher, 94
  IRC, 72-73
Clinton, Bill, 34, 50, 124
coin collectors mailing list, 46
colleges, Internet access through, 8
colon (:), 57
command(s). *See also* commands (listed by name)
  Gopher, 96
  IRC, 74-76
  lines, 22
  newsgroup navigation, 62
  Unix, 13, 21-24
commands (listed by name)
  attach commands, 41-42
  cd command, 37
  copy command, 23
  cp file command, 23
  Ctrl-C command, 22, 39
  Ctrl-G command, 25
  Ctrl-I command, 22
  Ctrl-J command, 41
  Ctrl-K command, 25
  Ctrl-O command, 25
  Ctrl-R command, 25
  Ctrl-T command, 41
  Ctrl-U command, 25
  Ctrl-W command, 25
  Ctrl-X command, 25, 38, 57, 63
  finger command, 29, 150
  Get All Newsgroups command, 124
  get command, 89
  ls -a command, 23, 56
  /join command, 75, 76, 77
  ls command, 82
  man topic command, 23
  mkdir command, 24
  more command, 24
  move command, 23
  /msg command, 75, 76
  mv file command, 23
  New Message command, 40
  newname command, 23
  /quit command, 75, 76
  ren command, 23
  rm filename command, 23
  rx filename command, 24
  rz filename command, 24, 41
  Send command, 35, 40
  Show All Newsgroups command, 55
  sx filename command, 23
  sz command, 23, 42, 82, 83
  uncompress command, 84
  V command, 41-42
comp newsgroups, 54, 136, 149
compressed files, 84
CompuServe
  basic description of, 16
  e-mail, 14, 41, 42
computer(s). *See also* Macintosh; PCs (personal computers)
  Amiga computers, 108
  mainframe computers, 4
  names, 30, 34, 81
copy command, 23
copyrights, 170
cp file command, 23
credit cards, 19, 103, 133-134
Crossing Guard, 132
C shell, 26, 154
.cshrc, 26-27

Getting Started

Ctrl key commands
  Ctrl-C command, 22, 39
  Ctrl-G command, 25
  Ctrl-I command, 22
  Ctrl-J command, 41
  Ctrl-K command, 25
  Ctrl-O command, 25
  Ctrl-R command, 25
  Ctrl-T command, 41
  Ctrl-U command, 25
  Ctrl-W command, 25
  Ctrl-X command, 25, 38, 57, 63
Cybersitter, 132

D

deleting
  current lines, 25
  e-mail messages, 39, 124
  files, 23
Delphi, 16
dial-up access
  basic description of, 8, 149
  FTP and, 82
dinosaurs mailing list, 46
direct connections, 9, 149
directories. *See also* home directory
  Archie and, 88-89
  creating subdirectories in, 24
  definition of, 149
  FTP and, 80, 82-84
  listing the contents of, 23
  names of, 81
directories, telephone/ e-mail, 137-138
discussion lists. *See* mailing lists
dollar sign ($), 10, 22, 29, 147
domain names, 12
DOS (Disk Operating System), 9-10, 22-23

directories, 22
prompt, 10
Down Syndrome mailing list, 47

E

EDITOR lines, 26-27, 63
editors
  Pico editor, 24-25, 36-38, 57-58, 63-64, 153
  vi editor, 24-25
e-mail. *See also* e-mail addresses; mailing lists
  AOL, 14
  attachments, 41-42, 137, 148
  body of, 35, 40
  CompuServe, 14, 41, 42
  cost of, 20, 135
  definition of, 149
  Elm program for, 35, 37-39, 40, 42, 124, 149
  example usage of, in "a day in the life," 138-140
  finding an Internet access provider and, 14-15, 18-19
  folders and, 36, 37, 39
  FTP through, 83-84
  getting "up to speed" on, 123-124
  MIME encoding and, 41-42, 152
  netiquette, 43-45, 66-67
  newsgroups and, 125
  overview of, 33-51
  Pine program for, 35-37, 39-42, 124, 153
  reducing long-distance phone bills with, 31
  saving, in directories, 26
  sending binary files through, 41-42
  shell accounts and, 10, 12
  signatures, 27-28, 148

Index

subject line of, 35, 40
typing credit card numbers into, 133-134
Unix and, 27
Usenet News and, 55
viruses and, 137
e-mail addresses. *See also* e-mail
  address books for, 37, 38, 40
  basic description of, 33-35
  directories/listings of, lack of, 137-138
  as FTP passwords, 81, 83
  getting familiar with, 124
Elm, 35, 37-39, 40, 42, 124, 149
elmrc, 37
encryption, 134
Eudora, 35, 39-41, 124, 167
  basic description of, 150
  binary attachments and, 42
exclamation point (!), 34, 57
exiting, the Pico editor, 25, 57, 63

F

FAQ (Frequently Asked Questions) file, 66, 67, 68, 150
ferrets mailing list, 47
Fetch, 81
file(s). *See also* files (listed by name)
  compressed, 84
  deleting, 23
  inserting, 25
  moving, from one directory to another, 23
  renaming, 23
  viewing long, 24
File menu, 109
file name extensions, 84-85

files (listed by name)
  .cshrc, 26-27
  elmrc, 37
  .newsrc, 56-61, 124, 147
  .plan, 28-29, 147
  .profile, 26-27, 63, 148
  .signature, 27-28, 148
finger command, 29, 150
fj newsgroups, 54
folders, in e-mail programs, 36, 37, 39
follow-up messages, 60, 63, 150
freeware
  definition of, 85
  e-mail programs, 35-36
Fruit-of-the-Day mailing list, 47
FTP (file transfer protocol), 10, 164
  Archie and, 87-89, 97
  basic description of, 18, 79-91, 150
  directories and, 26
  by e-mail, 83-84
  getting connected to the Internet and, 18, 19
  getting Eudora through, 40
  IRC and, 77
  mirrored sites and, 85, 152
  recommended sites, 85-86
  Usenet News and, 67
  using, overview of, 80-83
  the World Wide Web and, 104, 110-111
fungus mailing list, 47

G

games, 26, 29
genealogy mailing list, 48
Get All Newsgroups command, 124
get command, 89

171

Getting Started

GNN (Global Network Navigator), 114
Gopher, 12, 19, 30, 85
　Archie and, 89
　basic description of, 93-100, 150
　clients, 73, 94
　commands, 96
　getting "up to speed" on, 126
　Jewels, 98
　Jughead item, 97
　recommended sites, 97-98
　server, 94-95
　subject trees, 97-98
　using, overview of, 95-96
　the World Wide Web and, 101, 104, 207, 110-111
graphical interface. *See also* graphics
　e-mail and, 39-40, 42
　FTP and, 82
　graphical versions of Unix, 22
　IRC and, 73, 77-78
　newsreaders and, 58-59, 64, 65
　shell accounts and, 10
　SLIP/PPP connections and, 11
　Web browsers and, 108-112, 164-165
graphics. *See also* graphical interface
　Mosaic and, 164-165
　posting, in newsgroups, 64-65
Griffith, Andy, 48
Gulf War, 5
GZip, 84

H

hackers, 131
Hahn, Harley, 144
handles, 74, 150. *See also* nicknames
help

Gopher, 96
Internet Anywhere, 157
IRC, 75
newsgroup, 63
Unix, 23, 25
Web browser, 109
hierarchies, division of newsgroups into, 54-55, 150
hobbies, 31-32
Home button, 108
home directory. *See also* directories
　basic description of, 22, 151
　.plan file in, 28-29
　saving signature files in, 28
　Unix files in, 25-29
host names, 12, 151
hotlists, 110, 127, 151, 163-164
How To Connect, 19
HTTP prefix, 163
hyperlinks, 102, 163

I

IBM (International Business Machines), 5, 163
InterCon, 11
Internet. *See also* Internet access providers
　basic description of, 3-4, 151
　getting on the, 7-20
　getting perspective on, 129-138
　misconceptions about, 130-138
　types of access to, 9-13
　usage statistics for, 5-6
　the World Wide Web and, relationship of, 103
Internet access providers
　basic description of, 7-20, 151
　finding, 13-17

Index

picking, 17-19
rates of, 17, 18, 19-20, 135
Internet Anywhere, 11, 13, 39, 157-162
Internet Chameleon, 11
Internet Complete Reference, 144
Internet for Dummies, 144
Internet in a Box, 11, 13, 39
Internet Movie Database Web Page, 117
Internet Relay Chat. *See* IRC (Internet Relay Chat)
Internet Society, 86
internetwork, definition of, 5-6, 151
Internet World, 30, 80, 106, 109
 access to, on the World Wide Web, 115
 subscription information for, 143-144
IP (Internet Protocol) addresses, 12, 149, 151
IRC (Internet Relay Chat)
 basic description of, 71-77, 151
 clients, 72-73
 commands, 74-76
 getting "up to speed" on, 125-126
 servers, 72-73
ls -a command, 23, 56
Israel, 34

J

Japan, 20, 54
job-list mailing list, 47
/join command, 75, 76, 77
Jughead, 97

K

Kantor, Andrew, e-mail address for, 34
kids mailing list, 47
Korn shell, 26, 154

L

LANs (local area networks), 8, 151
Letterman, David, 45, 49
Line-Mode Browser, 105-107
License Agreement (IDG), 169-171
List, The, 14-15
listserv, 151. *See also* **mailing lists**
ls command, 82
LuckyTown mailing list, 48
Lycos Web Page, 113
Lynx browser, 105, 106-107, 109, 152

M

Macintosh, 8-12, 84
 deleting files with, 23
 directories, 26
 e-mail and, 39-40, 41, 42
 Fetch, 81
 FTP and, 81
 IRC and, 73, 77
 Unix and, 22
 Usenet News and, 58, 64
 the World Wide Web and, 104, 108
MacWeb, 108
mailing lists
 basic description of, 42-43
 e-mail netiquette and, 44-45
 of interest, list of, 45-61
 subscribing to, 124
mainframe computers, 4
man topic command, 23
MCIMail, 42
MecklerWeb iWorld Web Page, 114, 115

173

Getting Started

Michigan State University, 96
Microsoft. *See also* Windows (Microsoft)
  Microsoft Info, e-mail address for, 50
  Microsoft Network, basic description of, 16
Military technology, 3-4
MIME (Multipurpose Internet Mail Extensions), 41-42, 152
mirrored FTP sites, 85, 152
misc newsgroups, 54, 152
misconceptions, about the Internet, 130-138
MIT (Massachusetts Institute of Technology), 67, 86
mkdir command, 24
modems
  14.4-Kbps access with, 17-18
  basic description of, 152
  dial-up access and, 8-9
  speeds, 17-18, 19, 82
  Web browsers and, 108
Modems for Dummies, 19
more command, 24
Mosaic browser, 11, 103-104, 108, 134
  downloading, 112
  Enhanced, 158, 162-165
  sound player, 164-165
MOSAIC.INI, 108
move command, 23
movies. *See also* video
  posting, in newsgroups, 64-65
  Web site devoted to, 117
/msg command, 75, 76
multimedia. *See* graphics; movies; sound; video
mv file command, 23

N

names
  computer, 30, 34, 81
  directory, 81
  domain, 12
  file, 23, 84-85
  host, 12, 151
  nicknames, 40, 72, 74-76, 150
  usernames, 19, 81
Net-Happenings mailing list, 48
Netcom, 13, 16
netiquette, 43-45, 66-69, 125, 152
netmask, 12, 152
Netscape browser, 11, 103-104, 134
  downloading, 112
  as a graphical browser, 108-109
  SLIP/PPP connections and, 104, 108
network, definition of, 5
New Message command, 40
newname command, 23
news newsgroups, 54, 66-67
  news.announce.important newsgroup, 67
  news.announce.newusers newsgroup, 67
  news.answers newsgroup, 66
  news.newusers.questions newsgroup, 67
newsgroups. *See also* newsgroups (listed by type);
newsreaders
  basic description of, 54, 152
  choosing messages to read from, 62
  division of, into hierarchies, 54-55, 150
  of interest, list of, 68-69

Index

moderated, 55
navigating in, commands for, 62
netiquette, 125
Newsgroup Browser and, 55
posting binary files in, 64-65
replying to messages in, 63
sending messages in, 63-64
subscribing to, 55, 56-58, 63, 125, 154
newsgroups (listed by type)
  alt newsgroups, 54, 65, 133, 148
  ba newsgroups, 54
  biz newsgroups, 54
  clari newsgroups, 54
  comp newsgroups, 54, 136, 149
  fj newsgroups, 54
  misc newsgroups, 54, 152
  news newsgroups, 54, 66-67
  nyc newsgroups, 54
  rec newsgroups, 54-57, 67, 133, 140, 153
  sci newsgroups, 54-55, 153
  soc newsgroups, 54, 154
  talk newsgroups, 54, 154
.newsrc, 56-61, 124, 147
newsreaders
  basic description of, 55, 152
  "catching up" action and, 124-125
  reading news with, overview of, 58-61
  writing messages and, 125
New York City, newsgroups originating from, 54
New York Times, 101-102, 116
nicknames, 40, 72, 74-76, 150
nn newsreader, 59-60, 62-65
NNTP news servers, 13, 58, 152

NSF (National Science Foundation), 130-131, 133
NSFnet, 130-131, 133
nyc newsgroups, 54

O

objectivism mailing list, 48
OpenMarket Web Page, 116
Open Text, 157. *See also* Internet Anywhere
  contact information for, 158
  Web Index, 165
O'Reilly & Associates, 29, 114
OS/2, 108

P

packet switching, 4-5, 153
passwords, 73, 81
Pathfinder Web Page, 117
PCs (personal computers)
  file name extensions and, 84
  getting on the Internet and, 8
  receiving files from, 23-24
  Usenet News and, 58
  the World Wide Web and, 104
PDIAL (Public Dial-up Internet Access List), 14-15, 153
Pegasus, 36
percent sign (%), 10, 22, 34
Personal Favorites lists, 110
PGP (Pretty Good Privacy), 133
Pico editor, 24-25, 63-64, 153
  editing elmrc with, 37
  editing .newsrc with, 57-58
  Elm and, 36-38
  exiting, 25, 57, 63
pictures, posting, in newsgroups, 64-65

Getting Started

Pine, 35-37, 39-42, 124, 153
PKUnZip, 84
.plan, 28-29, 147
plus sign (+), 61, 75
POP accounts, 12-13, 39, 153
pornography, 131-132
Postal Service, 4-5, 33-34
pound sign (#), 75, 147
Procomm Plus, 10
Prodigy
   basic description of, 16
   e-mail, 14, 41, 42
   software, 13, 16, 17
.profile, 26-27, 63, 148
PSI (Performance Systems International), 16

Q

Qualcomm, 35, 39, 167. *See also* Eudora
Quanta mailing list, 48
Quarterdeck Web Page, 103
/quit command, 75, 76
quitting. *See also* exiting
   Gopher, 96, 126
   IRC, 75, 76
   the Line-Mode Browser, 106
   Lynx, 107

R

Rand, Ayn, 48
rec newsgroups, 54-57, 67, 133, 140, 153
Redford, Robert, 102
ren command, 23
RTFM site (rftm.mit.edu), 67, 86
rm filename command, 23
rn newsreader, 58-59
Roots-L mailing list, 48
RTFM site, 86
Russia, 3-4
rx filename command, 24

rz filename command, 24, 41

S

San Francisco Bay Area, 54
"Save modified buffer?" message, 38
Savetz, Kevin, 144
saving
   files, Pico command for, 25
   signature files, 28
schools. *See also* colleges; universities
   e-mail addresses for sites in, 34
   Internet access through, 8
sci newsgroups, 54-55, 153
scrolling, 62, 107
security issues, 133-134
Send command, 35, 40
serial lines, definition of, 10
servers
   Archie, 86
   chat, 72
   definition of, 154
   Gopher, 94-95
   IRC, 72-73
   NNTP news, 13, 58, 152
   "secure," 134
   SMTP mail, 12-13, 39-40, 154
shell accounts
   basic description of, 9-13, 18-19, 154
   e-mail and, 36-37, 41-42
   FTP and, 81, 83
   Gopher and, 98
   IRC and, 73, 76
   PSI and, 16
   SLIP/PPP connections vs., 11-13
   Unix and, 21
   Usenet News, 56-57, 58-59
   the World Wide Web and, 104

Index

shells, definition of, 26, 154
Show All Newsgroups command, 55
signature files, 27-28, 148
skeptics mailing list, 49
slash (/), 74, 81
SLIP/PPPs connections, 16-18, 64
  basic description of, 9, 10-13, 154
  e-mail and, 35-36, 39-41
  FTP and, 81, 82, 85
  Gopher and, 97
  IRC and, 73
  signature files and, 28
  software for, 11-13, 17
  Usenet News and, 58
  the World Wide Web and, 104, 108
SMTP mail servers, 12-13, 39-40, 154
soc newsgroups, 54, 154
sound
  players, 164-165
  posting, in newsgroups, 65
  the World Wide Web and, 104
Soviet Union, 3-4
spacebar, 60, 61, 62
spamming, definition of, 67, 154
Springsteen, Bruce, 48
Spry, 36, 55, 134
Stone Age, 3-4
Stout, Rick, 144
StuffIt, 84
subject trees, 97-98
subnet, 12
Sumex-Aim, 85
SurfWatch, 132
Sweden, 20, 135-136
switching, packet, 4-5, 153
sx filename command, 23
symbols
  <> (angle brackets), 60, 66

* (asterisk), 75
@ (at sign), 34, 147
: (colon), 57
$ (dollar sign), 10, 22, 29, 147
! (exclamation point), 34, 57
% (percent sign), 10, 22, 34
# (pound sign), 75, 147
+ (plus sign), 61, 75
/ (slash), 74, 81
Synergy, 11
system administrators, 8, 123
sz command, 23, 42, 82, 83

T

talk newsgroups, 54, 154
tango mailing list, 49
TCP/Connect II, 11
technical support, 19
telephone
  lines, serial lines as, 10
  systems, Internet vs., 19-20, 135-136
telnet
  Archie and, 87
  basic description of, 18-19, 29-30, 155
  Gopher and, 96
  IRC and, 73
  Unix and, 27, 29-30
  Usenet News and, 64
Terminal (Windows), 10
TimesFax Web Page, 116
tin newsreader, 59, 155
TopTen mailing list, 45, 49
Toyota, 94-95
trn newsreader, 59, 61-65, 155

U

undelete actions, 23, 25
unencoding, 65
United Kingdom, 34
universities, 5, 8, 94, 95, 96, 113

University of Minnesota, 94, 95
Unix
  Archie and, 87
  "bang" in, 57, 147
  basic description of, 21-30, 155
  commands, 13, 21-24
  e-mail and, 35-42
  files, important, 25-29
  FTP and, 81, 82
  getting connected to the Internet and, 9
  Gopher and, 95
  IRC and, 72-73, 125
  Pico editor, 24-25, 36-38, 57-58, 63-64, 153
  prompt, 10, 22, 29
  shell accounts and, 10, 11
  uncompress command, 84
  Usenet News and, 56, 59, 60, 61, 124
  the World Wide Web and, 106
Unix in a Nutshell, 29
URLs (uniform resource locators), 109-110, 162-163
  basic description of, 104-105, 110, 155
  for recommended Web sites, 112-120
URouLette Web Page, 115
Usenet News, 15-16, 18-20, 80. *See also* newsgroups
  basic description of, 53-69, 155
  finding Internet access providers through, 15
  getting "up to speed" on, 124-125
  netiquette, 66-69
  the NEWS prefix and, 164
  pornography and, 132
  reading news with, 58-61

  Unix and, 27-28
  the World Wide Web and, 104, 106, 110, 112
usernames, 19, 81
Utah, 4
UUencoding, 42, 155

V

V command, 41-42
Veronica, 93, 97, 126, 155
VersaTerm-Link, 11
video, 84, 104
vi editor, 24-25
viruses, 136-137

W

Walnut Creek CD-ROM FTP site, 164
WANs (wide area networks), 155
Washington University, 85
waterski mailing list, 49
Web browsers. *See also* Web browsers (listed by name)
  basic description of, 104-105, 148
  getting "up to speed" on, 126-127
  secure servers and, 134
  text browsers, 105-107
  viewing Gopher menus with, 95-97
Web browsers (listed by name)
  Cello browser, 108
  Line-Mode Browser, 105-107
  Lynx browser, 105, 106-107, 109, 152
  MacWeb browser, 108
  Mosaic browser, 11, 103-104, 108, 112, 134, 158, 162-165
  Netscape browser, 11, 103-104, 108-109, 112, 134

Index

WinWeb browser, 108
WebCrawler, 114, 127
WebCrawler Web Page, 114
Web pages (listed by name)
  Internet Movie Database Web Page, 117
  Lycos Web Page, 113
  MecklerWeb iWorld Web Page, 114, 115
  OpenMarket Web Page, 116
  Pathfinder Web Page, 117
  Quarterdeck Web Page, 103
  TimesFax Web Page, 116
  URouLette Web Page, 115
  WebCrawler Web Page, 114
  Yahoo Web Page, 113
WebWeek, **115**
"What's On Tonite" mailing list, 49
"White Pages," 137-138
Windows (Microsoft)
  e-mail and, 39-40, 41
  FTP and, 81
  getting connected to the Internet and, 8, 10-12
  IRC and, 73, 77
  Terminal, 10
  Usenet News and, 64
  the World Wide Web and, 108
WinSock FTP, 81, 167
WinWeb, 108

word processors, 35
World Wide Web, 19, 30. *See also* Web browsers; Web pages
(listed by name)
  Archie and, 89
  basic description of, 101-119, 156
  getting "up to speed" on, 126-127
  hotlists and, 110, 127, 151, 163-164
  pornography and, 132
  secure servers on, 134
  usage, example of, in "a day in the life," 139-141
WUArchive, 85

X

Xmodem protocol, 23-24

Y

Yahoo, 113, 127, 140
Yahoo Web Page, 113
Your Internet Consultant: The FAQs of Life Online, 144

Z

Ziff-Davis Press, 19
Zmodem protocol, 23-24
ZTerm, 10

Colophon

This book was composed on Gateway 2000 P4-66, Gateway 2000 P5-75, and IBM ThinkPad 360CSE computers. All three used Microsoft Word for Windows 6.0c. Screen captures were taken with JASC Inc.'s Paint Shop Pro. Internet connection software was provided by Spry Inc. (later CompuServe Inc.). Additional products were provided from Netscape Communications Corp. (Netscape Navigator), Qualcomm Inc. (Eudora), John A. Junod (WinSock FTP), and Khaled Mardam-Bey (mIRC).

Internet connections provided by IBM and Public Access Networks Corporation (Panix). Cookies by Nabisco. ;-)

IDG BOOKS WORLDWIDE LICENSE AGREEMENT

Important — read carefully before opening the software packet. This is a legal agreement between you (either an individual or an entity) and IDG Books Worldwide, Inc. (IDG). By opening the accompanying sealed packet containing the software disc, you acknowledge that you have read and accept the following IDG License Agreement. If you do not agree and do not want to be bound by the terms of this Agreement, promptly return the book and the unopened software packet(s) to the place you obtained them for a full refund.

IDG Books Worldwide Licence Agreement

1. License. This License Agreement (Agreement) permits you to use one copy of the enclosed Software program(s) on a single computer. The Software is in "use" on a computer when it is loaded into temporary memory (i.e., RAM) or installed into permanent memory (e.g., hard disk, CD-ROM, or other storage device) of that computer.

2. Copyright. The entire contents of this disc and the compilation of the Software are copyrighted and protected by both United States copyright laws and international treaty provisions. You may only (a) make one copy of the Software for backup or archival purposes, or (b) transfer the Software to a single hard disk, provided that you keep the original for backup or archival purposes. The individual programs on the disc are copyrighted by the authors of each program respectively. Each program has its own use permissions and limitations. To use each program, you must follow the individual requirements and restrictions detailed for each in the Guide to Included Software at the back of this Book. Do not use a program if you do not want to follow its Licensing Agreement. None of the material on this disc or listed in this Book may ever be distributed, in original or modified form, for commercial purposes.

3. Other Restrictions. You may not rent or lease the Software. You may transfer the Software and user documentation on a permanent basis provided you retain no copies and the recipient agrees to the terms of this Agreement. You may not reverse engineer, decompile, or disassemble the Software except to the extent that the foregoing restriction is expressly prohibited by applicable law. If the Software is an update or has been updated, any transfer must include the most recent update and all prior versions. Each shareware program has its own use permissions and limitations. These limitations are contained in the individual license agreements that are on the software discs. The restrictions include a requirement that after using the program for a period of time specified in its text, the user must pay a registration fee or discontinue use. By opening the package which contains the software disc, you will be agreeing to abide by the licenses and restrictions for these programs. Do not open the software package unless you agree to be bound by the license agreements.

IDG Books Worldwide Licence Agreement

4. Limited Warranty. IDG Warrants that the Software and disc are free from defects in materials and workmanship for a period of sixty (60) days from the date of purchase of this Book. If IDG receives notification within the warranty period of defects in material or workmanship, IDG will replace the defective disc. IDG's entire liability and your exclusive remedy shall be limited to replacement of the Software, which is returned to IDG with a copy of your receipt. This Limited Warranty is void if failure of the Software has resulted from accident, abuse, or misapplication. Any replacement Software will be warranted for the remainder of the original warranty period or thirty (30) days, whichever is longer.

5. No Other Warranties. To the maximum extent permitted by applicable law, IDG and the author disclaim all other warranties, express or implied, including but not limited to implied warranties of merchantability and fitness for a particular purpose, with respect to the Software, the programs, the source code contained therein and/or the techniques described in this Book. This limited warranty gives you specific legal rights. You may have others which vary from state/jurisdiction to state/jurisdiction.

6. No Liability For Consequential Damages. To the extent permitted by applicable law, in no event shall IDG or the author be liable for any damages whatsoever (including without limitation, damages for loss of business profits, business interruption, loss of business information, or any other pecuniary loss) arising out of the use of or inability to use the Book or the Software, even if IDG has been advised of the possibility of such damages. Because some states/jurisdictions do not allow the exclusion or limitation of liability for consequential or incidental damages, the above limitation may not apply to you.

7. U.S. Government Restricted Rights. Use, duplication, or disclosure of the Software by the U.S. Government is subject to restrictions stated in paragraph (c) (1) (ii) of the Rights in Technical Data and Computer Software clause of DFARS 252.227-7013, and in subparagraphs (a) through (d) of the Commercial Computer—Restricted Rights clause at FAR 52.227-19, and in similar clauses in the NASA FAR supplement, when applicable.

Groovin' on the NET
with MKS INTERNET ANYWHERE™
for Windows

SPECIAL PRICE $49.00

You can be groovin' on the Net in minutes with Internet Anywhere. It's all the most powerful Internet tools in one fun easy-to-use package. Surf the World Wide Web with our Genuine Mosaic™ browser • exchange e-mail faster and easier with our feature packed mail program • tune into thousands of newsgroups with MKS news • even upload information with our drag and drop FTP. But this is just the beginning! From the Internet Anywhere desktop, you have everything at your fingertips, including a multimedia learning center to show you all the right moves so groovin' on the Net is fast, fun, and easy (the way the Internet was meant to be). Purchase MKS Internet Anywhere now on CD-ROM (MSRP $79) by visiting your local computer store, book store, or Internet access provider. Or call toll free 1-800-507-5777 and

GET READY TO GROOVE THE NET WITH INTERNET ANYWHERE!

MKS and MKS Internet Anywhere are trademarks of ... ems Inc. All other trademarks acknowledged. Outside of North America order line: 1 (519) 88... ...es@mks.com, WWW: http://www.mks.com

GENUINE MOSAIC

OPEN TEXT WEB INDEX™

The Only Address You Need to Find Everything on The World Wide Web!

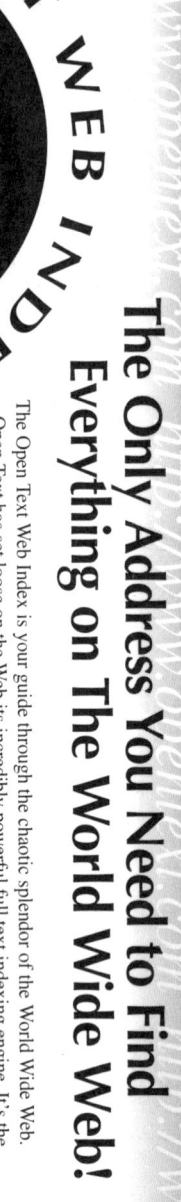

The Open Text Web Index is your guide through the chaotic splendor of the World Wide Web. Open Text has set loose on the Web its incredibly powerful full text indexing engine. It's the fastest most comprehensive search engine available on the Web today, and it's **FREE**! A "web crawler" is continuously visiting every home, nook and cranny on the Web, noting every word—adding the new documents, and updating the index as they change. Millions of documents. Tens of millions of links. Billions of words. Use your Web browser to visit the Web Index "home page", type in the words or phrase you're looking for—and instantly ALL the documents containing those words are listed. The Web Index then helps you to narrow the focus quickly. All this is FREE to any Internet user. No limits. No subscriptions. No "professional version" that charges you for the power you actually need. And all of this is backed by a Web site that is professionally cared for and maintained by UUNET. Visit the Web Index "home page" at *http://www.opentext.com* and discover the most valuable tool on the Internet today!

OPEN TEXT CORPORATION

180 Columbia St. W.
Waterloo, ON Canada N2L 3L3
Marketing (519) 888-9910
Fax (519) 888-0677
Email info@opentext.com

http://www.opentext.com

Plug In and Turn On!

The Portal Information Network™ is the best kept secret on the Internet! We provide Internet service for individuals, businesses, educational institutions and research facilities. For the past 10 years, Portal® has been the leading nationwide Internet dialup provider.

Worldwide Coverage and Roaming Internet Accounts

Portal has more than 1,100 local access numbers. This makes us the most widely accessed nationwide Internet access provider. And with so many access numbers, no matter how far you roam you are generally never farther than a local call away from service. Portal's Automatic Account Creation allows you to easily access the Internet in less than 60 seconds using a local access number.

Special Rates!

For Internet Anywhere™ customers who have chosen Portal as their Internet access provider. We offer a US$15.00 credit towards Internet service. After the intial 30 day trial period, the monthly rate is only US$9.95. The local access charges are US$2.95/hr in the US including Alaska and Hawaii, and US$3.95/hr in Canada and Puerto Rico.

PORTAL

The Portal Information Network
20863 Stevens Creek Blvd., Suite 200
Cupertino, CA 95014 USA
408.973.9111 (voice) 408.725.1580 (fax)
sales@corp.portal.com (email)
http://www.portal.com

Portal is a registered trademark of Portal Information Network, Inc. Other trademarks are property of their respective owners. Copyright ©1995 Portal Information Network Inc. All rights reserved.

Here's Your Chance to Start a No-Risk Trial Subscription to Internet World . . .

The Only Magazine Focused Exclusively on Helping You Navigate the Internet

FREE TRIAL ISSUE!

Here's your chance to send for a No-Risk Trial Subscription to Internet World, the only magazine focused exclusively on helping you navigate the Internet. Whether you're new to the Internet or a seasoned user, Internet World gives you all the information you need to make the most of your time on the Internet. Each issue brings you:

- tips on using the Internet's various search and retrieval tools.
- expert commentary on new services and resources.
- interviews with Internet luminaries and exciting coverage of technical, legal, commercial, and social aspects of the Internet.

For advanced users, Internet World brings a compelling blend of news, features, columns, tips, how-to articles and personality, and vendor profiles. For beginners, there's the Entry Level column aimed at helping "newbies" connect to the Internet and navigate its resources.

Mail the attached TRIAL SUBSCRIPTION voucher today and take advantage of this risk-free offer!

TRIAL SUBSCRIPTION VOUCHER

☐ **Yes**, please enter my risk-free trial subscription to Internet World! If I'm not completely satisfied with my first issue, I'll write "cancel" across your first invoice, return it and owe nothing at all. Otherwise, I'll pay just $19.97 for a one-year (12 issues) subscription— an incredible 66% savings off the annual newsstand cost.

☐ 1 year (12 issues) only $19.97 ($39.43 off the newsstand costs.)
☐ 2 years at only $39.94 (Double my savings!)

Name ☐ Mr. ☐ Mrs. ☐ Ms. _____
Address _____
City/State/Zip _____
(City/Province/Postal Code)

E-mail address _____
(optional)

☐ Payment enclosed   ☐ Bill me later
Rate in the Americas (other than U.S.) $44.00 (includes postage and Canadian GST).
Allow 6-8 weeks for delivery of first issue.

AIDG95

internet WORLD

Master the Internet with Internet World

The Most Widely Read Magazine Devoted Entirely to the Internet

Despite all you've read and heard about the Internet, there's only one magazine focused exclusively on helping you navigate the Internet—Internet World. And now you can save 66% on the magazine that everyone's talking about:

> "Recommended."
> PC Magazine, March 1994

> "A regular infusion of Internet ideas. The magazine covers a full range of Internet services..."
> The New York Times, June 1994

> "You'll most likely want to subscribe..."
> Information Today, June 1994

Whether you're new to the Internet or a seasoned user, INTERNET WORLD gives you all the necessary information to make the most of your time on the Internet—tips on using the various search and retrieval tools, expert commentary on new services and resources, exciting coverage of technical, legal, commercial, and social aspects of the Internet. So subscribe today!

NO POSTAGE NECESSARY IF MAILED IN THE UNITED STATES

BUSINESS REPLY MAIL
FIRST CLASS MAIL   PERMIT NO. 282   MT. MORRIS, IL

POSTAGE WILL BE PAID BY ADDRESSEE

internet WORLD™

P.O. Box 713
Mt. Morris, IL 61054-9965

☐ **YES!**
Please keep me informed about IDG's World of Computer Knowledge. Send me the latest IDG Books catalog.

BUSINESS REPLY MAIL
FIRST CLASS MAIL   PERMIT NO. 2605   FOSTER CITY, CALIFORNIA

IDG Books Worldwide
919 E Hillsdale Blvd, STE 400
Foster City, CA 94404-9691

NO POSTAGE
NECESSARY
IF MAILED
IN THE
UNITED STATES

IDG BOOKS WORLDWIDE REGISTRATION CARD

RETURN THIS REGISTRATION CARD FOR FREE CATALOG

Title of this book: Internet World 60 Minute Guide to the Internet Including the World Wide Web

My overall rating of this book: ☐ Very good [1] ☐ Good [2] ☐ Satisfactory [3] ☐ Fair [4] ☐ Poor [5]

How I first heard about this book:
☐ Found in bookstore; name: [6]
☐ Book review: [7]
☐ Advertisement: [8]
☐ Catalog: [9]
☐ Word of mouth; heard about book from friend, co-worker, etc.: [10]
☐ Other: [11]

What I liked most about this book:

What I would change, add, delete, etc., in future editions of this book:

Other comments:

Number of computer books I purchase in a year: ☐ 1 [12] ☐ 2-5 [13] ☐ 6-10 [14] ☐ More than 10 [15]

I would characterize my computer skills as: ☐ Beginner [16] ☐ Intermediate [17] ☐ Advanced [18] ☐ Professional [19]

I use ☐ DOS [20] ☐ Windows [21] ☐ OS/2 [22] ☐ Unix [23] ☐ Macintosh [24] ☐ Other [25] _____ (please specify)

I would be interested in new books on the following subjects:
(please check all that apply, and use the spaces provided to identify specific software)

☐ Word processing: [26]
☐ Spreadsheets: [27]
☐ Data bases: [28]
☐ Desktop publishing: [29]
☐ File Utilities: [30]
☐ Money management: [31]
☐ Networking: [32]
☐ Programming languages: [33]
☐ Other: [34]

I use a PC at (please check all that apply): ☐ home [35] ☐ work [36] ☐ school [37] ☐ other: [38]

The disks I prefer to use are ☐ 5.25 [39] ☐ 3.5 [40] ☐ other: [41]

I have a CD ROM: ☐ yes [42] ☐ no [43]

I plan to buy or upgrade computer hardware this year: ☐ yes [44] ☐ no [45]

I plan to buy or upgrade computer software this year: ☐ yes [46] ☐ no [47]

Name: _____ Business title: [48] _____ Type of Business: [49]

Address (☐ home [50] ☐ work [51] /Company name: _____

Street/Suite#

City [52]/State [53]/Zipcode [54]: _____ Country [55]:

☐ **I liked this book!** You may quote me by name in future IDG Books Worldwide promotional materials.

My daytime phone number is _____

IDG BOOKS

THE WORLD OF COMPUTER KNOWLEDGE